David Cannistraci has been pastoring ... a thriving local church with healthy leaders and healthy teams. This book is written in a style that promotes practical implementation and ideas for building teams. It's a book that every church can use on every level to invite conversations on how to build together. The six conversations are proven to be wise and usable. It's my privilege to totally, 100% endorse David and this book.

—**Dr. Frank Damazio**
Chairman, Minister Fellowship International
Author of The Making of a Leader, Strategic Church and Life
Changing Leadership

I've worked with a lot of pastors over the years, and I've seen every possible style of leadership imaginable. But every now and then I meet a pastor who has such a shepherd's heart that I say to myself, I wish I could work for him! That's how I feel about my friend David Cannistraci. This book explains why. David knows that real leadership is about teamwork. He believes the best leader is willing to empower others so that they surpass him. Rather than pursuing a self-focused agenda, a true leader includes his whole team in the process. I believe *Let's Talk About Teams* will make you a better leader, and it will unify and strengthen the people who lead with you.

—**J. Lee Grady**
Director, The Mordecai Project
Author, *Set My Heart on Fire*

If you are serious about building great teams, I highly recommend *Let's Talk About Teams.* My friend David Cannistraci has given us an invaluable tool. It's brief, biblical, practical, and is designed for immediate real-life application with your team.

—**Chip Ingram**
CEO/Teaching Pastor, Living on the Edge

I love my friend David Cannistraci's new book *Let's Talk About Teams*. This is not just another book on leadership. It is packed with practical wisdom for healthy team building that releases great influence and a godly leadership legacy for the next generation. Leaders and teams from many walks of life will find this book to be an extraordinary tool for building healthy teams through trust, unity and relationship. David's writing comes from many years of experience as he has modeled these truths and walked in humility, wisdom and integrity. I highly recommend you read this book!

—**Larry Kreider**,
International Director, DOVE International

I have known David Cannistraci for many years. I have watched him use the principles in his book to build a thriving and successful church. He is not only an excellent pastor, but he is an amazing coach. Anyone using the principles that he has laid out in *Let's Talk About Teams* will not only grow their church but will experience an amazing retention of key people. It is my honor to not only endorse him as a long-time friend, a pastor of great excellence; but to endorse his book as a practical and spiritual guide to an excellent ministry.

—**Dr. Sanford "Sandy" G. Kulkin, PhD.**
CEO, PeopleKeys, Inc.
Chairman of The Bair Foundation
President of Institute of Motivational Living

One of the first things Jesus did when beginning his earthly ministry was to choose a team. He was showing us the way to have exponential impact with the collective TOGETHER. In this book David gives us a strong theological base AND practical conversations to have in order to make healthy teams a reality in our churches. Just imagine what forces our churches could be if we paid deep attention to this.

—**Nancy Ortberg**
CEO, Transforming the Bay with Christ

Pastor David Cannistraci, like Paul in the New Testament, is a master builder, an apostle who has been anointed by God to lay down foundations - in his case for city-wide pastoral unity. In *Let's Talk About Teams,* he shares with agile prose, garnished with real life examples and personal testimonies, the wisdom that God has entrusted to him through many years of faithful and inspiring service locally and globally. He is not a theoretician but a practitioner of what he teaches. I have known him for decades and the aroma of Christ constantly flows out of him. I can testify from first hand experience that the San Francisco Bay Area has been greatly blessed and enriched by his ministry. I enthusiastically recommend this book because it will enable you to facilitate the healthy unity among leaders that is critical for the world to believe.

—**Dr. Ed Silvoso**
Founder and CEO of Transform Our World
Author, *Anointed for Business* and *Ekklesia*

Let's Talk About Teams is an exceptional book, releasing the grace of a wise master builder (1 Corinthians 3:10). My friend, David Cannistraci helps us recognize and apply principles to see powerful kingdom connections made through *teams.* This causes the passion of the Lord and the need in our culture to be met. This is a great book filled with wisdom, insight and revelation to take our organizations to new levels of effectiveness.

—**Robert Henderson**
President of Global Reformers
Bestselling Author of *Operating In The Courts Of Heaven* and the
Court of Heaven Series

Over the decades, I have been privileged to work with some of the finest team builders in the body of Christ. Furthermore, I have read countless books on the vital subject. What distinguishes a great leader from all others in their field is the one who first models what he teaches and THEN teaches what he modeled. David Cannistraci is one of those rare leaders who has spent decades forging team-building principles in the furnace of his own ministry context and

THEN eloquently hammered them into a genuine invaluable leadership tool called, *Let's Talk About Teams*. This instrument of pure gold stands high above the rest and I would highly recommend this book for both your personal use and the use of all your leaders.

—Pastor Marc Estes
Lead Pastor City Bible Church
President Portland Bible College

In this practical book, David Cannistraci masterfully describes how to put together effective teams in ministry to help bring God's kingdom to earth. He provides many insightful ways to maneuver inevitable pitfalls as well as shows how to help team players make their best contributions in order to arrive at the goals they set to accomplish. It is packed with many colorful illustrations that add punch to his points. Besides, it is uncomplicated and fun to read!

—Doris M. Wagner
Widow of Dr. C. Peter Wagner

If you are looking to develop greater synergy in your teams and organizations, I believe that *Let's Talk About Teams* will be a powerful resource for you. Grounded in biblical principles, this book gleans from years of experience in building strong team ministries. Unlock the power and potential of teamwork through the practical handles and guiding questions offered by Pastor David Cannistraci. Dare to believe that your leadership and teams can change for the better!

—Reverend Dominic Yeo
Secretary, World Assemblies of God Fellowship
General Superintendent, The Assemblies of God of Singapore
Senior Pastor, Trinity Christian Centre

David Cannistraci is a leader among leaders. Ministry has been his focus throughout his entire life. His teachings have been important to thousands. His church has grown to become a great example of health and strength in the world today, in part because of his understanding of building healthy leaders and healthy teams. Now, he shows us how to do it as well. I recommend this book to your and your leadership team.

—**Dr. Emanuele Cannistraci**
Founding Pastor GateWay City Church
San Jose, California

I am always on the lookout for leadership growth opportunities, especially from practitioners who are living out what they talk about. David Cannistraci is one of those leaders I seek out and learn from. His work here will guide you not only to grow as a leader but the book is organized in such a way that the leadership gets passed on to teams that you work with. He is practical, specific, thorough and brings a wealth of experience with leading a church and living a godly life to each element he shares.

It's always wise to read great books and even wiser if you can see the reality of what the book is claiming to help you with. *Let's Talk About Teams* is written for pastors and leaders who are in a local church context. This is a church building book with a focus on leaders and teams.

—**Pastor Steve Clifford**
Lead Pastor, WestGate Church
San Jose, California

Dr. David Cannistraci is passionate about making us all better. He believes that we can all be more purposeful and fruitful. He knows that leaders make the world go round and the best leaders build healthy teams to capture and sustain success.

Let's Talk About Teams is a smart, intelligent, balanced, highly practical book to help you and your team become healthy, fruitful and successful. It is a no-nonsense, level headed guide to leading and supporting the people around you to be their best and accomplish more than ever.

Dr. Cannistraci lives what he writes. His life and fruitful ministry are a testament to authentic, healthy leadership and team-building. I've watched him for decades. He's the real deal. His principles shared in this book actually work and are doable for anyone committed to bettering themselves and those around them. Read this book and grow. Apply this book and bring the best out in others you've been assigned to. Everyone wins with the truths in *Let's Talk About Teams.*

—**Pastor John Chandler Cleveland**
Global Impact Group

It's true: Teamwork makes the dream work. I heartily recommend this book no matter what chapter of your Christian walk you are currently in. David Cannistraci has been on to this kingdom principle for a long time. Learn the power of moving from a measure of grace to grace without measure. None of us is as powerful as all of us.

—**Dr. Ed Delph**
NationStrategy, Phoenix, Arizona

In *Let's Talk About Teams,* David Cannistraci brings both solid theology and seasoned wisdom on how a church can have maximum impact for the kingdom. It is born out of the many years of experience of one of Silicon Valley's most effective leaders and pastors. I am always on the lookout for resources that are solid in their biblical foundation and user friendly for use in the local church setting. This is one of those resources. It will not only enrich the individual who reads it, but will also be a great tool for raising the level of leadership wherever it is used. I highly recommend it.

—**Pastor Ken Foreman**
Lead Pastor, Cathedral of Faith
San Jose, California

David Cannistraci's new book, *Let's Talk About Teams* is an invaluable, insightful book focused on how to develop healthy teams in very practical ways yet with great stories that were inspiring to me. This book was both insightful and challenging when discovering the principles and attributes of healthy teams. This is a must read for all pastors and leaders who want to build healthy teams.

—**Pastor Justin Manzey**
Latitude Ministries
www.latitudeministries.com

Dr. David Cannistraci has written a superb, practical, must read book for all pastors and spiritual leaders. His writing is shaped by many years as an experienced, seasoned, and effective pastor leading a significant church. I recommend *Let's Talk About Teams* to all of our networks.

—**Dr. Joseph Mattera**
National convener, United States Coalition of Apostolic Leaders
Overseeing Bishop of Christ Covenant Coalition

Pastor David Cannistraci has written a guide to building ministry teams that has long been needed. This frank, well-researched book demonstrates ways to build trust and agreement, even in challenging situations. Commitment to the principles David shares will bless your ministry teams today and generations of your church members tomorrow.

—**Dr. Caroline Ward Oda, PhD**
Chancellor, Transformation University
Transform Our World

It is absolutely true—teamwork makes the dream work. The power and value of healthy team relationships and dedicated synergistic collaboration are inestimable to achieving dreams and visions. Everyone is important. Everyone really matters.

In *Let's Talk About Teams,* Dr. David Cannistraci has done a masterful job presenting practical insights to help you build effective, sustainable teams that are keys to fruitful ministry. David is my friend and brother. He's an amazing man and a phenomenal leader. I'm convinced this book will bless your life and ministry. It will be a must read for Agape leaders and teams.

—Dr. Lawrence Powell
Lead Pastor Agape Family Worship Center
Rahway, New Jersey

It is an honor having Pastor David as a friend and fellow-leader for more than three decades. His life and leadership are a rare integration of charismatic vitality and intellectual maturity, all aimed to glorify God and expand God's kingdom through the mission of the local church. His new book, *Let's Talk About Teams* is a compact, intense and practical guidebook for health in the local church, with application to any community or organization. This is not a work for someone that wants "three easy steps" to success. It is a challenging and dense resource that will inform thoughtful leaders for the long haul. I hope it finds wide readership...and even more importantly, application. In an era of stressed-out leaders and morally-broken systems, David's book offers a fresh vision for community vitality.

—Dr. Charlie Self
Director of City Expansion, Made to Flourish
Professor of Church History,
Assemblies of God Theological Seminary
Author of Flourishing Churches and Communities

David Cannistraci seized my attention early on with an African proverb: 'If you want to go fast, go alone. If you want to go far, go together.' This book is all about going far by refining our relational skills to better 'go together.' You'll especially appreciate the scholarship, analogies, gripping examples, and real life experience in the trenches...Remarkable!

I have always admired the teachings of Pastor David because they are invariably honest, real, clear—and practical. On several occasions, I have asked Pastor David 'May I just sit in your staff meetings and observe?' And when I attended, I would sit in a corner, observe how he interacts with and leads his team, and take notes. Team building is one of David's strengths and I am so glad he is sharing his insights, knowledge, wisdom, and experience with us through this book.

One of the greatest God given resources of the local church is the concept of team. Woven within the heart of each individual, are God given resources to accomplish his purposes, build his church and extend his kingdom. Unfortunately, the resources buried within the heart of a team can be easily overlooked and in some instances never excavated.

In *Let's Talk About Teams,* Pastor David does a masterful job in providing practical tools to help churches and leaders bring out the gold God has placed deep in the vault of their collective hearts and minds. This rich resource will be a valuable tool to help you and your team flourish in God's purpose for your life and church.

David Cannistraci's latest book, *Let's Talk About Teams* is packed with practical strategies for doing life and ministry successfully as a team. As great as we might be, we cannot accomplish what God has called us to as a lone-ranger. He did not design us to be independent but interdependent- in need of connection with Him and each other.

"This incredible book is a must-read for anyone who wants to develop and build relationships and teams as God ordained. It will equip you with practical tools to help you navigate your relationships with others in your work to accomplish His purpose and assignments for your lives and ministry. At the end of each chapter you will find an excellent 'Leadership Takeaway' and exercises to guide your personal reflections or stimulating conversations in small group towards building healthy teams. I highly recommend this book to the body of Christ!

—**Dr. John A. Tetsola, Senior Minister**
Ecclesia Word Ministries International
Bronx, NY

Whenever I get around Pastor David Cannistraci, it is impossible to not feel encouraged, challenged and infused with hope for the future. He is a leader of leaders, and this book is a treasure chest of time-tested principles and strategies that will take you and your team to the next level. From the moment I picked up this book, I couldn't put it down. Speaking from years of experience, Pastor David shares practical and relevant principles of how to lead more effectively. I feel that my personal leadership 'metron' has grown because of this book, and I only wish it had been around when I first started this adventure of leading people. This is a must read for leaders and teams!

—**Pastor Jonathan Wilkins**
Lead Pastor, City Life Church
San Francisco, California

DAVID CANNISTRACI

LET'S TALK ABOUT TEAMS

SIX SIGNIFICANT CONVERSATIONS TO BUILD YOUR TEAM AND HELP YOU FLOURISH IN MINISTRYTOGETHER

CONTENTS

Dedication   1
Gratitude   3
Introduction   5

CONVERSATION #1: *Why Teams Matter*   9
Talk It Over   24
Team Up and Make It Better   25
Leadership Takeaway   26

CONVERSATION #2: *The Beauty of Relationships*   29
Talk It Over   46
Team Up and Make It Better   48
Leadership Takeaway   49

CONVERSATION #3: *There's No Team Without Trust*   53
Talk It Over   72
Team Up and Make It Better   73
Leadership Takeaway   74

CONVERSATION #4: *The Symphony of Team Agreement* 81
Talk It Over   101
Team Up and Make It Better   103
Leadership Takeaway   104

CONVERSATION #5: *Even Heroes Need Training*   109
Talk It Over   130
Team Up and Make It Better   132
Leadership Takeaway   133

CONVERSATION #6: *New Tools for Team Building*   137
Talk It Over   162
Team Up and Make It Better   164
Leadership Takeaway   165

Epilogue   170
About the Author   179
Notes   181

DEDICATION

This book is dedicated to the pastoral leadership team of GateWay City Church. You guys put in the *teamwork* to make the *dream work* every week in every city where we serve. Many of you have been by my side for decades. How can I say thanks? Without your faithfulness, energy, prayers, and brilliant gifts, we would never have come this far. Your achievements and your struggles have inspired me, touched me, and kept me grounded. Kathy and I are honored to be on the same team with each of you.

GRATITUDE

It takes a team to write a book about—-teamwork. Amy Fyfe was my editor, and Pastor Colleen Brown was the driving force behind the discussion questions. She assisted with editing as well. These two make me look much better than I am. Kathryn Kong is a gifted writer who made helpful suggestions. Thanks ladies, let's do this again!

GateWay's staff team helped me think through the questions and needs of my readers. They have great minds and hearts. I love our Tuesday equipping times together. Our creative team helped me with the title and other elements. My son, Pastor Jordan Cannistraci, designed the cover, and Pastor Chris Cobb helped me with formatting and preparation for publication amid a family emergency—his commitment was truly "second mile." My amazing wife Kathy was patient with my extra hours away from her and supportive of this entire project. Huge thanks to each of you.

I also gratefully acknowledge Carey Nieuwhof's *Lasting Impact* (Cumming, GA: The reThink Group, Inc., 2015) first inspired me to organize the chapters of *Let's Talk About Teams* around discussion times aptly named "Conversations." He writes an excellent church leadership blog at CareyNieuwhof.com.

Most of all, I am grateful for God's unending grace. It is real, and I have learned that I can't live without it. Thank you Lord—more please!

INTRODUCTION

I believe in the church. I'm not talking about *my* church, but *the* church. The church is not an abstract religious idea, human organization, or physical location. The church is nothing less than the billions of broken people all over the world who have been redeemed through faith in Jesus Christ, filled with His resurrection life, and who are being organized as His instrument to advance His eternal kingdom.

The church began as small and unimpressive—barely 120 people huddled together in a small upper room, trying to imagine their uncertain future. They had limited training, no investors but themselves, little start-up money, and only a vague concept of their mission. Their leaders were mostly the uneducated, disadvantaged, and despised inhabitants of a largely ignored corner of the first-century Roman world. Their world was filled with superstition, idolatry, political injustice, and growing persecution.

Yet the church grew and flourished like nothing else in human history. It spread through city after city until it filled the known world. This happened because the church was, and always will be, supernatural—it was fueled with love and miracles, and its leaders worked together and sacrificed everything to see it advance. Today, the church is the most phenomenal movement of people the world has ever seen.

I love the church, and nothing is more important to me than to see it flourishing and advancing. And while I recognize that the church is not always what it needs to be, it remains the only thing that Jesus ever said He would build (Matthew 16:18). The world is literally transformed as Jesus builds His church, and I can think of nothing more important than being a part of this magnificent process.

I have written this book out of a passion to see the church flourish. When I wrote my first book, *Apostles and the Emerging Apostolic Movement,* [1] and my second book, *God's Vision for Your Church,* [2]

5

I had the same goal in mind. *Let's Talk About Teams* is a third effort to strengthen the church that I love by teaching, encouraging, and hopefully inspiring its leaders and members to do great things.

There are scores of great books on healthy leadership and church growth, and there are a number of solid books on team ministry—so why another? Not many have been written for the staff and volunteer level reader. Most have focused on the executive levels of leadership—the boards, executives, and senior leaders of large churches. *Let's Talk About Teams* is written to help the next level leaders in their week-to-week efforts to build healthy teams in churches and ministries.

Hopefully this is more than a book—it is intended to be a tool. The right conversations can inspire results, so I have arranged this material to help catalyze discussion and application. Each of the six "Conversations" consists of a chapter with important ideas about healthy team ministry. The *Talk It Over* sections guide the reader through a group discussion. The *Make it Better* section provides ideas for applying what has been learned, and the *Leadership Takeaway* section is intended to create value for team leaders.

This book is not intended to be an exhaustive work on this topic. It is written as an introduction to the subject for the widest possible audience. I have attempted to be academically sound without boring or weighing my readers down with useless theory. I hope I have succeeded in creating a readable, inspiring tool to help people flourish together in ministry.

My hope is that *Let's Talk About Teams* will help solve problems and create benefits for my readers by helping them to understand how to get more done with less effort. There is too much burnout and too little results in many churches. There are too few workers and not enough time. We can make this better by looking at things differently and working together in healthy teams.

Dr. David Cannistraci
September 2018

WHY TEAMS MATTER

*"You can do what I cannot do. I can do what you
cannot do. Together, we can do great things."*
—MOTHER TERESA

In the summer of 2018, millions around the world watched and held their breath. News reports were lighting up the airwaves about a young boys' soccer team trapped deep in a flooded cave complex in northern Thailand. The boys had been on a team-building exercise deep inside an intricate system of connected caves when a sudden rainstorm flooded their exit route, cutting them off from the outside world and making any rescue extremely difficult. Time was quickly running out. The possibility that these helpless children and their coach would face starvation, suffocation, or drowning terrified everyone.

The Thai government quickly deployed a team of their own Navy SEALs, but almost immediately, one of their most skilled operators drowned in a heroic attempt to save the boys. The Thais realized that they were literally in over their heads. Diving in the turbulent, murky channels between the flooded caves was simply beyond their skill set, and getting the children—most of whom could not swim—back out through those obstacles would be impossible unless they got help.

The call went out to a special group of Brits who had spent decades training for just such an emergency. They also welcomed skilled operators from Australia, Britain, China, Laos, Myanmar, and the United States. In the end, it was the teamwork between the Thais and their international partners, all working together in a series of daring operations, which led to the rescue of all twelve boys and their coach. The world breathed a collective sigh of relief and saw another vivid demonstration of the power of a team.

Big things happen the moment we say, "Let's do this together."

What would happen if you received some help with the most important challenges in your life? What if, instead of struggling alone in your family, ministry, and professional life, you could team up with a trusted partner or two by your side? What if there was a way to make our churches and ministries more powerful, more fruitful, and more healthy as they reached people for eternity?

LET'S TALK ABOUT TEAMS

In this book, you will find six important conversations that have the potential to change your life for the better. Whether you are a leader or a behind-the-scenes person in business, education, government, or ministry, the power of teamwork can unlock new possibilities.

- In Conversation #1, we're starting with the WHY. Why should we pursue teamwork in our lives? What are the most compelling reasons for doing life and ministry as a team? It's amazing what benefits we can experience when we open up and begin doing things together.

- In Conversation #2, we'll talk about healthy relationships. Everyone needs help with relationships, and the Bible is the best place to find it. We'll discover how relationships are meant to work on healthy teams and the "tumbler of the team" that God uses to get us to that goal.

- In Conversation #3, we'll learn the importance of building trust from mountain climbers. In this broken world, how can we trust others? How can we earn the trust of those around us? Those answers can lead to healthier families, teams, and churches.

- In Conversation #4, we'll discover the power of agreement and learn the secrets of a symphony conductor. There is nothing more rewarding than building agreement on the purpose, values, and direction of our lives. When it comes to being a healthy leader or building a healthy team, agreement is a total game changer.

- In Conversation #5, we'll turn our attention to the art of investing in a team. As the Navy SEALs know, every team needs to be trained. Are there simple, effective ways to add value to others so we can win battles together? We'll share some ideas for mining the potential of your team.

- Finally, in Conversation #6, we will wrap our journey up with practical direction for building healthy teams. Life is not about what you know, it's about what you do. This conversation will get us thinking and acting together about what tools we can use to build healthy teams.

I encourage you to absorb this small book together with a group of friends, family members, or ministry partners. Dive in to the stories and principles. Meet together for six weeks and have healthy conversations based on the chapters and accompanying discussion questions. Think deeply about who God has called you to be and what He has placed in your heart to do. Pray together and help each other make the adjustments that need to be made. Do it together, and you will see the power of these principles first hand.

WHAT IS A TEAM?

Many dictionaries define a team simply as "two or more people working together." A fuller definition might be "a group of people with different skills and roles who work together on a common project." Jon Katzenbach and Douglas Smith, in their book *The Wisdom of Teams,* define a team as "a small number of people with complimentary skills who are committed to a common purpose, performance goals, and approach for which they hold themselves mutually accountable." [3]

An African proverb says, "If you want to go fast, go alone. If you want to go far, go together." This highlights the potential of teamwork to take us further in life than we can go by ourselves. That is the essence of teamwork: coming together to reach a goal that none of the team members could reach by themselves. In other words, when we team up, we can accomplish great things together.

Whatever definition you choose, *together* is the operative concept. Without the core value of getting things done *together*, you have no team and no real win.   As the one and only Babe Ruth once said, "You may have the greatest bunch of stars in the world, but if they don't play together, the club won't be worth a dime."

Together means we are no longer working alone. Our tendency to "go it alone" is often our undoing in life. Years ago, I read a funny story about the foolishness of working alone. It's about a bricklayer who was trying to move a 500-pound load of bricks from the top of a building down to the sidewalk below. Unfortunately, he paid a painful price for working alone, as his account of the incident on his employer's insurance form reveals.   John Maxwell retells the story as well as anyone:

> "It would have taken too long to carry the bricks down by hand. So I decided to put them in a barrel and lower them by a pulley, which I had fastened to the top of the building. After laying the rope securely at the ground level, I then went up to the top of the building. I fastened the rope around the barrel, loaded it with the bricks, and swung it out over the sidewalk for the descent.
>
> Then I went down to the sidewalk and untied the rope, holding it securely to guide the barrel down slowly. But, since I weigh only 140 pounds, the 500-pound load jerked me from the ground so fast that I didn't have time to think of letting go of the rope. And as I passed between the second and third floors, I met the barrel coming down. This accounts for the bruises and

lacerations on my upper body. I held tightly to the rope until I reached the top, where my hand became jammed in the pulley. This accounts for my broken thumb.

At the same time, however, the barrel hit the sidewalk with a bang and the bottom fell out. With the weight of the bricks gone, the barrel weighed only about 40 pounds. Thus, my 140-pound body began a swift descent, and I met the empty barrel coming up. This accounts for my broken ankle. Slowed only slightly, I continued the descent and landed on the pile of bricks. This accounts for my sprained back and broken collarbone. At this point, I lost my presence of mind completely and let go of the rope. The empty barrel came crashing down on me and caused my head injuries.

As for the last question on the form, 'What would you do if the same situation arose again?'—Please be advised that I am finished trying to do my job alone." [4]

Laughable, right? Except that it is too often an accurate picture of us. Why do we try to get things done by ourselves? The results are too often painful. God never intended us to work alone, war alone, or walk alone. Doing things as a team makes far better sense.

The Bible has a lot to say about the word *together*. For example:

"All the believers were *together* and had everything in common. They sold property and possessions to give to anyone who had need. Every day they continued to meet *together* in the temple courts. They broke bread in their homes and ate *together* with glad and sincere hearts, praising God and enjoying the favor of all the people. *And the Lord added to their number daily those who were being saved."* ACTS 2:44-47 NIV

"(Christ) makes the whole body fit *together* perfectly. As each part does its own special work, it helps the other parts grow, so that the whole body is *healthy and growing* and full of love." EPHESIANS 4:16 NLT

13

God's plan has always been that His people would experience His purposes and His power together. On the most powerful day in the history of the church—the day of Pentecost in that upper room in Jerusalem—the power of the Holy Spirit was poured out as the church was "together in one accord" (Acts 2:1). In fact, if you removed the word *together* from the New Testament, there would be no power, no church, no fellowship, no health, no impact, and no growth at all!

"Together" is both a spiritual and practical game-changer!

What makes *together* so special is that it can work in every arena of life. When we do life and ministry as a team, more needs will be met. People can be happier and healthier when they are doing things together. Fewer of us will get burned out or left out. And just like the early church found, God can add to the church in greater numbers.

SUPERNATURAL SYNERGY

One of the most amazing advantages of doing life and ministry as a team is often overlooked. Healthy teams carry the dynamic power of synergy. Synergy means the potential of two or more parts coming together is greater than the potential of the individual parts alone. On a team, this means that when two or more people or organizations combine their efforts, they can get more done together than they can in isolation. Over time, synergy can multiply and yield exponential results.

I once heard about a horse-pulling competition, where the winning horse was able to pull around 5,000 pounds of dead weight while the second place horse pulled around 4,000 pounds. After the event was over, out of curiosity, the organizers paired the two horses together to see how much they could pull as a unit. Many expected that they would be able to pull around 9,000 pounds together, which makes sense because of simple addition. What actually happened was when the two horses pulled together, they were able to move nearly 12,000 pounds! That's natural synergy.

Supernatural synergy is available in our lives. For example, when we team up in prayer, the Lord releases His power:

> "Again, truly I tell you that if two of you on earth agree about anything they ask for, it will be done for them by my Father in heaven. For where two or three gather in my name, there am I with them." MATTHEW 18:19-20 NIV

This seems to run parallel to the supernatural victories God promised Israel when they came together to fight for the Lord:

> "Five of you will chase a hundred, and a hundred of you will chase ten thousand, and your enemies will fall by the sword before you." LEVITICUS 26:8 NIV

Are you pulling alone or fighting alone in life? If the missing ingredient in your life is supernatural synergy, then teaming up in life and ministry could be the answer. Even a small team can experience great victories together—just ask Gideon (see Judges 7). When we do things together, our synergy releases creativity, new ideas, personal growth, and bottom-line results. In church, that could mean more prayers answered, more people reached, more families healed, more churches planted, more songs written—the list goes on and on. Can any of us really afford to overlook the power of synergy to make things easier?

TEAMING UP FOR GOD

The power of teamwork is often seen in sports where championships are either won or lost based on how well the players work together. In the business world, profits and growth ultimately depend on the proficiency of the many teams involved. In the military, teams are utilized to overcome obstacles and win battles; the most elite units in the world are composed of the strongest teams. Schools and universities have discovered the power of small groups and cohorts to serve as ideal learning environments, bringing *together* into the classroom. Even something as simple as a family camping trip can be harmonious or become disastrous, based on whether or not family members work together as a team. Everywhere you look in life, people understand the importance of teamwork.

How about in the church—Do we understand teamwork? Are we experiencing multiplication within our faith communities, or are subtraction and division more common? As we've seen, the concepts of togetherness in life and ministry were a normal part of life in the early church. But there is also a crystal clear pattern of team ministry throughout both the Old and New Testaments.

- *The Trinity:* The Bible reveals God as three united, yet distinct, persons—Father, Son, and Holy Spirit. [5] There aren't three Gods; there is only one God (Deuteronomy 6:4). The Father is God (Philippians 1:2), the Son is God (John 1:1,14), and the Holy Spirit is God (Acts 5:3-4). So in God's very nature, divine teamwork is operating.

- *Moses and the Elders:* The number of people Moses was trying to help was wearing him out. His father-in-law, Jethro, chided him for failing to utilize the power of teamwork (Exodus 18:13-26). When Moses built a team of faithful leaders to help him, his load was lightened, and Israel became healthier. In your own life, don't be tempted to lead alone. God has placed good people all around you as a resource.

- *The Wisdom of Solomon:* According to the wisest man who ever lived, no one should ever work or war alone. "So don't go to war without wise guidance; victory depends on having many advisers" (Proverbs 24:6). Our best strategies emerge from a team of godly counselors. Life is a huge battle, and we face lots of enemies, but if we can war together, we can win together.

- *Jesus and the Twelve:* Teamwork was Christ's core strategy from the very beginning. In Matthew 10, we see that He began his short three-and-a-half year ministry by calling and assembling a team that would carry on His work once He had departed.

Jesus understood that the future of the church would depend on this team. As His followers, we should have no other aim.

- *The Seventy:* Jesus sent His disciples out in teams of two (Mark 6:6-7, Luke 10:1). Why? He understood that people learn, grow, and function better when they are together. His method has profound implications for us. If the greatest leader of all time made teamwork a centerpiece of His plan from the beginning, can we justify doing less?

- *Paul and Barnabas:* The book of Acts reveals a pattern of teamwork. The clearest example of this was in the sending of Paul and Barnabas (Acts 13:1-3, 13-14). As a diverse team of prophets and teachers prayed and fasted, God brought Paul and Barnabas together as an apostolic team. Hands were laid on them and they were sent to plant churches. Over time, the teams morphed and other teams were formed, but the pattern in Acts was always a team working together.

- *The Body of Christ:* Paul referred to the church as "the body." He chose the human body as an analogy of the value and connection of every member on the team, saying "Just as our bodies have many parts and each part has a special function, so it is with Christ's body. We are many parts of one body..." (Romans 12:4-5, NLT). The work of God has no room for independent contractors. Whether we are leaders who equip or members who are engaged in ministry, we are a team working together for the good of all (Ephesians 4:11-17).

Teamwork is a God-thing! We have been given a clear pattern of teamwork in God's Word, but it is up to us to "build according to the pattern God has given us" (Hebrews 8:5).

BARRIERS TO TEAMWORK

If teaming up is so powerful, why do so many of us fail to do it? Why do good people who love God and long to see great things happen so often "go it alone" in life? The answer boils down to faulty mindsets that undermine our potential. Here are five of the most common struggles we face on the way to doing life and ministry together:

- *We might be self-reliant.* Children often proclaim their maturity, saying "I can do it myself!" It's great to see children wanting to be independent, but when it comes to living as an adult, there is no room for childish ways. Healthy people cannot live completely *independent* of each another. Neither should healthy people live completely *dependent* on others. Instead, God's plan is for us to live in *interdependence*—where we live and work together, each of us committed to doing our part, and receiving from others and building up the whole as one (Ephesians 4:16).

- *We might be scared.* Have you ever felt insecure about stepping out and trying something risky? Doing life and ministry as a team can challenge our secret fears: "What if no one wants to help me? What if I mess up and get it wrong? It's safer to just keep doing it alone." Doing things together may mean a loss of control or freedom, and for most of us, that is unnerving. Yet when we get others involved, we can gain so much more than we lose. It is true that working with others exposes us to the risk that we might be hurt, challenged, or taken advantage of. But without a team, we get none of the benefits either. All relationships require risks, but in the end, love generates overwhelming returns.

- *We might be stressed.* Many of us might think, "I agree with the importance of building teams, but I just don't have the energy." Believe me, I get it. Between kids, work, ministry, appointments, cleaning our house, making meetings, etc. we are all so rushed in life that it feels like we can't add another thing. That is a common struggle, especially for leaders. Here's how I encourage my team: Even a small change can make a big difference. You don't have to get there overnight. Just make a few key adjustments in the way you do things and trust God. Small tweaks can take you to major peaks, and in the end, you'll have less stress, not more.

- *We might be self-focused.* Every one of us is capable of hidden pride. For example, in writing this book, I asked my team to give me some feedback on my chapters. Boy, did they! As their critiques and suggestions piled up, I was honestly tempted to stop asking for their help. Involving them was challenging me as a communicator and pinching my secret pride. Have you ever experienced that? The problem with hidden pride and self-focus is that it will eat our lunch every time. What if those Thai Navy SEALs had insisted on saving those twelve boys by themselves? Doing life and ministry as a team means stepping back and opening up to something greater and larger than ourselves.

- *We might be stuck.* I heard one time about an older man who went to the doctor because his wife suspected that he was suffering with hardening of the "categories". If you are a pastor, boss, husband, mother, student, worker, or wife, may I ask you: Are you stuck in a rut? Maybe you just keep doing things a certain way because that is the way you've always done them. How's that working for you? If you want things to get better, you need to try a new approach. God calls us to restructure our thoughts, habits, and commitments in order to bring about real life changes. He wants to get us unstuck and release His new wine by giving us fresh, new wineskins (Luke 5:37-39).

*When we change our minds about how we get
things done, we'll experience huge rewards.*

We all get off track in our thinking. Our mindsets rob us of the joy of experiencing the best things in life. There is a better way: instead of surrendering to the ideas that limit us, we can change the way we think. That is called *repentance*, and it leads to incredible blessings.

EIGHT BLESSINGS OF TEAMWORK

The wisest man who ever lived brilliantly summarized the benefits of teamwork:

> "Two people are better off than one, for they can help each other succeed. If one person falls, the other can reach out and help. But someone who falls alone is in real trouble. Likewise, two people lying close together can keep each other warm. But how can one be warm alone? A person standing alone can be attacked and defeated, but two can stand back-to-back and conquer. Three are even better, for a triple-braided cord is not easily broken." ECCLESIASTES 4:9-12 NLT

Success, safety, warmth, victory, and strength are big benefits. As we come to the end of this chapter, let's consider eight concrete advantages of doing life and ministry as a team.

1. Teamwork accomplishes more.

Doing life and ministry as a team multiplies what we can accomplish. When we do life and ministry alone, we can only get so much done. We hit the ceiling on results when we work by ourselves. With the element of teamwork, more people are involved and far more is accomplished. Imagine an army of one fighting an army of one thousand—who is going to win? Ask any single parent if his or her life would be better with a helpful team. When we do life and ministry together, more people can be reached, more lives can be changed, and more battles can be won.

2. Teamwork makes things easier.

When we do life and ministry with others, everyone is more rested because, as my father used to say, "Many hands make light work." I remember the time Kathy and I had to move out of our first apartment, and I only had one person to help me. It was so discouraging, and it took forever. From that day on, whenever I've had to move, I make sure to get plenty of help lined up! Burnout and discouragement are common challenges we all face in our everyday lives, but teamwork is a great way to stay encouraged, rested, and balanced.

3. Teamwork affords more opportunity.

Teamwork multiplies our potential by raising the number of people that can get involved. This is a big benefit to a church or ministry leader, but it is also crucial for the people themselves. When people have a chance to make a contribution, they gain a sense of significance, belonging, and self-worth. They are literally a part of the team, and that can be a profoundly healing experience. When we allow others to help by creating a slot for them, we are helping them to flourish emotionally and spiritually. When we refuse to share the load, we rob them of life. Doing life and ministry as a team unlocks hidden potential, fills our ministry pipeline, and increases everyone's sense of ownership.

4. Teamwork releases everyone's best.

Teamwork often allows people to specialize in what they are good at. Everyone is a "10" somewhere! For example, on a baseball team, some are great pitchers, while others are better fielders or batters. The more positions we open up and the more people we get involved, the easier it becomes to discover their talents and best positions. In a one-man operation, the bases can never be covered. Things can fall through the cracks. Imagine going in for a major surgery and finding there was only one guy on the surgical team! The specialization of a full medical staff, including a surgeon, anesthesiologist, and a team of nurses, is the only way to pull off a lifesaving operation. It takes a team of specialists each doing their individual jobs together accurately.

5. Teamwork creates a buffer of safety.

Teams make each of us healthier and stronger because when you increase participation, you invite protection: "...For in the multitude of counselors there is safety" (Proverbs 11:14). Have you ever been blind-sided by something you didn't see coming? I have learned the hard way to listen to my family and my team before making a major move. When thinking and acting alone, one can misread a situation and make mistakes. We all have blind spots, but when we have a team of people around us with diverse gifts, experiences, and perspectives, we always end up in a better position. There is safety in numbers, and this is one of the most tangible benefits of doing life and ministry as a team.

6. Teamwork increases our satisfaction.

There is something so satisfying about being a part of a community, partnering up and accomplishing important things with people that you really love. Living for ourselves is depressing, but living for a bigger purpose gives us a break from our selfishness and allows us to experience a satisfying life. Getting more done in less time brings more joy and fulfillment to everyone on the team. Celebrating wins and processing losses together is also profoundly comforting, and is only possible when we open up to the team concept.

7. Teamwork leaves a legacy.

When we do things together, we extend the lifespan of our impact. My wife Kathy teases me because I love shopping at Walmart. The prices are so low it makes me giggly! But did you know that Walmart has become a multi-generational business powerhouse that has grown to become our nation's largest private employer? Team building was one of Walmart founder Sam Walton's best skills. From the beginning of his family-run store in Arkansas in the early 1960s, Sam invested in his team. Decades later, Sam Walton's heirs are among the richest people in the world. This legacy reminds us that when we behave as a one-man show, the show can die with us, but when we build a healthy team, things can carry on long after we are carried off. [6]

8. Teamwork invites God's power.

Kathy and I have a team of intercessors who pray for us on a regular basis, and it has changed our lives. We experience less stress, resistance, and spiritual attacks in our life and ministry because there is strength in numbers. King David observed,

> "How good and pleasant it is when God's people live together in unity! It is like precious oil poured on the head, running down on the beard, running down on Aaron's beard, down on the collar of his robe..." PSALM 133:1-2 NIV

He understood that God supernaturally empowers teamwork. There is something so empty and lifeless about doing life and ministry by our selves. But on a team, God releases unstoppable spiritual power and blessing!

What could happen if each of us saw our church or ministry as a kind of rescue team, something like the one that saved those twelve boys in Thailand? We are surrounded by multitudes of lost people. The dark currents of sin and evil hold them captive and only Christ's love and power can save them. As the church, we are the hands and feet of Jesus Christ, but time is running out. The evil one is working against us, the challenges ahead are complicated, and the stakes are high. How can we reach the lost?

The answer involves us coming together to form teams. We can do this *together*. We can experience the supernatural synergy and power of God in every area of our lives through teamwork. The pattern in Scripture is clear, but unless we overcome our mistaken mindsets and receive a fresh new wineskin, we will lose our opportunity. Whether it is in life, ministry, or relationships, none of us can do it alone, but when we work together, we can accomplish anything!

Conversation #1

TALK IT OVER

After you've read the Chapter on WHY TEAMS MATTER, take a few minutes with your group to talk through some of the questions below. Give everyone a chance to share, and encourage everyone to be honest, authentic, and supportive of others. Always remember to affirm vulnerability and thank those who are willing to share and ask for prayer.

1. Everyone has feelings of insecurity, stress, and discouragement. When it comes to doing life and ministry as a team, what emotional battles do you face, and how do they affect your life?

2. You may have watched the development of the cave rescue in Thailand via the media. International cooperation of this degree is rare. What do you think inspired people to put aside their differences and rise to this level of international teamwork? How do you think the mission of the church compares to the Thai rescue mission?

3. Have you ever been on a team where you thought it might be easier to just do it all yourself? Did you ever end up following through on this approach? If so, what eventually happened to the team? When this happens frequently, it is usually a leadership problem rather than a team problem. What underlying issues does the "do it yourself" leadership style reveal?

4. What about time limitations—How big a role does that play in your life? How can we find the time to get started together as a real team? What might happen if we don't?

5. Remember the two horses pulling together? Do you ever feel like you are pulling alone in life? Why? How have you experienced

the power of synergy in your life? How can we help each other overcome the temptation to carry the load alone?

6. Teamwork helps groups accomplish more, but it also brings tremendous personal blessings. What are some of the potential benefits produced in individual team members when they are given an opportunity to be involved?

Conversation #1

TEAM UP AND MAKE IT BETTER

Before you end your group conversation...

- Review these tips for getting started on the journey toward healthier teams together: Don't get overwhelmed. Trust that God is leading you, and He will help you move toward His plan for your ministry at the right pace. Start small and get everyone on board. Remember, there is no such thing as a perfect team, and it's okay to make mistakes together.

- Affirm each other personally. Let someone else in your group know why you admire them and believe in them.

- Take a few minutes to pray together about the opportunity to become more of a team, believing that when we pray together, Jesus is present and promises to answer our prayers.

Sometime before your next conversation...

- Review this chapter and note anything that you've decided to change in your life. Talk to God about it, and make a decision to get started by faith.

- Read the next chapter so you'll be ready to have a great conversation when your group gets together next.

LEADERSHIP TAKE-AWAY #1:

"Healthy Leaders Build Healthy Teams"

Teams matter, especially when it comes to the role of a leader. If you are leading a family, group, or ministry, you are so important to God, and what you do as a leader really matter for others. Please consider why moving forward into a greater role as a team builder would be a game-changer for you and those who depend on you.

- *Team building is a smart leadership strategy.* Not only is teamwork a clear pattern of ministry in the Bible, it really works. What makes teamwork such a powerful concept for the church is that a team operates in both *relational dimensions* and *functional dimensions.* In other words, a team both relates together and works together. That is exactly what you as a leader are called to do! Small groups are essential for creating and supporting healthy relationships in a church, but teams add another vital component: *getting something done for God.* Teams bring us into both *high relationship* and *high function* in the church. That makes teaming up for God incredibly relevant for leaders today.

- *Team building is a leader's main assignment.* Peter Drucker has said, "The successful leaders are those who know their job is to build an effective team that will outlast them." [7] Leaders who are making an impact pay attention to selecting their teams, connecting with their teams, building their teams, and utilizing their teams to make the church healthy and effective. Healthy leaders work at cleaning out unhealthy mindsets. Healthy leaders strive to build a culture of teams and team players on every level of their ministry. Healthy leaders also admit that they can't do what they are called to do by themselves, and they see teamwork as a core value in their calling.

- *Team building is a prophetic priority.* Let me say this prophetically—One of the most important trends of the coming decade will be a massive shift toward team ministry as a primary methodology in the body of Christ. No church or ministry can be healthy or effective apart from the principles of teamwork. The past decades of the church, which have often been characterized as being led by highly gifted but stand-alone leaders, have produced a tragic legacy of wasted lives and resources. The day of the one-man ministry is over. God is raising up churches and teams to get His work done in these last days.

- *Team building is a personal imperative.* If I may also speak to you personally by the Spirit of God, teams are imperative in your ministry. My friend, please don't miss this in leadership: you may never fully realize God's incredible plan for you as a chosen instrument until you embrace and implement the revelation of teams into your life and ministry. Don't pass these concepts off as though they don't apply to you or cannot work for you. You are a crucial part of God's plan, and this is your time to overcome your fears and exhaustion. You are destined to go to the next level in your ministry, becoming a healthy leader surrounded by healthy teams!

Conversation #2

THE BEAUTY OF RELATIONSHIPS

"Three things remain: faith, hope, and love—yet love surpasses them all. So above all else, let love be the beautiful prize for which you run."
—THE APOSTLE PAUL

Steve Jobs was the iconic visionary who helped launch and lead Apple towards becoming one of the most successful businesses on the planet. I live and serve in the heart of Silicon Valley—and I own way too many Apple devices—so I have a very real appreciation for his astounding accomplishments.

One of his most famous stories involves a man in his eighties who lived up the street from Jobs when he was young. One day, the older man invited him into his garage to show him an improvised rock tumbler that consisted of a coffee can, a small motor, and the rubber band which connected them. The older man then escorted Jobs to his backyard where they collected some ordinary rocks. Together, they placed them into the tumbler with a little liquid and a touch of gritty powder. The older man closed the can, switched the motor on, and invited Jobs to come back the next day.

Jobs recalled the terrible noise those stones made as they tumbled around on each other and how he couldn't wait to come back and see the results of the tumbling process. The next day, they opened the can, and Jobs was amazed: those ordinary rocks were now polished and attractive. Over time, the friction between the stones hadn't broken them—it had created something beautiful.

"Teams," Jobs would often say, "are like these stones. Individually we can be fairly normal, ordinary, and even a bit rough. But through the process of teamwork we can end up in a very different state."

Healthy relationships are the core of a healthy team.

In our first conversation, we focused on the potential of healthy teams to accomplish great things. One of the questions we might ask in measuring a team's health is, *Are they low-functioning or high-functioning?* In other words, are they getting important things done together? But healthy teams need to be more than highly functional—they need to be *highly relational* as well. In this conversation, let's look at relationships and how they affect our teams, and then talk through some ideas about creating healthier relationships in our family lives, work lives, and ministry lives.

LIFE IS ALL ABOUT CONNECTING

When it became clear that the passengers aboard the hijacked planes on September 11, 2001 wouldn't survive, many of them instinctively reached for their mobile phones to call their loved ones. Their carefully chosen words sent messages about the importance of loving connections: "I love you...I'm so lucky to have married you...Tell the kids Daddy loves them." None of them said, "Don't forget to water the lawn" or "Be sure to take care of my golf clubs." Their messages focused on relationships, because our relationships are among the most beautiful gifts in life.

When God wants to bless us, He gives us relationships. When He saw Adam alone, He gave him Eve. When He saw each of us lost in sin, He gave us Jesus. And when He sees our potential to grow and become what He has designed us to become, He gives us each other. Relationships are also God's delivery system. Everything He wants to give us comes through the conduit of a relational connection. Without those connections, these gifts can never arrive in our lives as God intends.

These kinds of gifts never come cheaply. Great marriages, friendships, families, and teams require sacrifice and selflessness. The more effort we put into our relationships, the more beauty we can experience and the healthier we can grow. Over time, the rewards for staying in the tumbler with those we love release an unexpected beauty—we are polished and perfected in the process.

Some time ago, I was counseling Marcus and Cindy, a couple who came in ready for a divorce. Marcus was frustrated, Cindy was desperate, and both of them were out of answers. As we talked, Marcus admitted feeling that he just wasn't "good at relationships." Cindy wept as she shared that she had never had a single healthy relationship in her life. They were willing to build a healthy relationship, but they simply had no clue how to do it. They are not alone.

Everyone struggles with relationships.

Some of my most painful struggles in life and ministry have involved something going wrong in a relationship. I've made many mistakes in my relationships, and while I have made amends and tried to heal where possible, the memories of my mistakes still sting. How about you? I'm willing to bet that both the lowest and highest points in your life were related to something going on within a relationship.

Trend-watchers are noticing that Americans are in something of a "relational famine." Polls consistently reveal that we are lonely and feeling more and more isolated in our fast-paced culture. We are spending more time trapped in cars, cubicles, and in front of our electronic devices and less time connecting with people. As a result, we have fractured families, dysfunctional teams, broken churches, and a generation of relationally malnourished people.

The church has been created to be a spiritual family for believers. The Bible says, "God places the lonely in families; He sets the prisoners free and gives them joy" (Psalm 68:6). Our relationships can be a living demonstration of God's restoring love in the midst of a broken world. The central icon of our faith—the cross of Jesus

Christ— is a visual representation of a relational reconciliation with God (the vertical dimension), and a relational reconciliation with each other (the horizontal dimension). The message of the cross is revealed as both dimensions come together (1 John 2:9-11). Healthy relationships should be one of the defining characteristics of any church, family, or true follower of Jesus.

THE GLUE THAT HOLDS US TOGETHER

What does it take to experience healthy relationships? As Marcus and Cindy listened, I explained that genuine love is the glue that holds our relationships together. I turned my attention to Marcus, saying, "You can't hold your marriage together with anger, fear, and control. Those ugly tactics are damaging your wife and ruining this relationship."

I then encouraged Cindy, who was wiping her eyes with a tissue. "There is a way to make this work. The Bible is a book about love and the power of love to keep us close to God and close to each other. Let's look to God's Word together and discover what He says about having healthy relationships." I wanted them to understand that there was hope for their relationship, but that without the glue of love, no relationship can avoid coming apart.

So how can we define love? Almost 40 years ago, I was a Bible college student studying in the shade of the giant Redwood trees of Scotts Valley near the California coast. Rev. Dick Foth was teaching us from 1 Corinthians 13—Paul's famous treatise on love. He said something that I had to write in the margin of my Bible:

"Love is the accurate estimation and adequate supply of another person's need."

Love, he said, is not a feeling, it is an action—a commitment to make another person's needs a personal priority. For example, parents love their children, so they meet their children's needs. Husbands love and are called to meet the needs of their wives. God personifies love (1 John 4:8). He saw our need of forgiveness and so loved us that He sent Jesus to meet our greatest need. God's love for each of us is eternal, unconditional, and unstoppable in meeting our needs.

One day, an expert in religious law tested Jesus with a question. "Teacher, which is the greatest commandment in the Law?" Perhaps he was thinking that the greatest law would be something related to tithing, the Sabbath, or eating a ceremonially appropriate diet. Jesus gave a reply that has forever defined who God is and what He requires:

> "'Love the Lord your God with all your heart and with all your soul and with all your mind.' This is the first and greatest commandment. And the second is like it: 'Love your neighbor as yourself.' All the Law and the Prophets hang on these two commandments." MATTHEW 22:36-40 NKJV

For Jesus, everything God ever revealed through Moses and the prophets boiled down to two simple things: loving God and loving people.

Life is all about who we love and how well we love them.

On another occasion, as the evening sky grew pink with the setting of the sun, Jesus sat with His disciples around a table in an upper room in Jerusalem. They were not far from a hill called Calvary where He would soon offer Himself as a sacrifice for the sins of the world. What would be the subject of His final words to His team?

> "So now I am giving you a new commandment: Love each other. Just as I have loved you, you should love each other. Your love for one another will prove to the world that you are my disciples." JOHN 13:34-35 NKJV

The law of love would be the only glue that would hold His Kingdom-building team together.

Love is the power that moves us.

Love motivates us like nothing else. Pastor Wayne Cordeiro tells how his cross-country coach trained runners. "Your first priority is simply this: to love running...If you run because you love running, you'll run and run and run." He was right. If you don't love to run, you'll soon quit. But if you love it, you'll never stop. Love has the power to move us toward the things that matter most.

As Marcus and Cindy stared blankly at me, I asked them a question. "What if serving God together could be so freeing and enjoyable that we'd never give up, even in the hard times? It can be," I said, "if we have love empowering us." The Bible says "Jacob worked seven years in return for Rachel, but *the years seemed like only a few days to him because he loved her*" (Genesis 29:20, GWT). If we do things out of obligation, ego, or ambition, it feels lifeless and empty. But if we do things out of love, life will be enjoyable and purposeful.

Paul the apostle revealed what motivated his entire ministry: "For Christ's love compels us..." (2 Corinthians 5:14-15, NIV). The JB Phillips translation reads, "The very spring of our actions is the love of Christ." In other words, love can be the nuclear power plant for all of life and ministry. That is why, in another place, Paul encouraged us, saying, "Let love be your highest goal!" (1 Corinthians 14:1, NLT). Doing things together for God requires us to "keep the main thing the main thing," and the main thing is love. If a family or team lacks love, it is certain to come unglued.

BIBLICAL PEOPLE-SKILLS

The lights were starting to turn on in Marcus and Cindy's minds, so I got more practical. "Love begins as a set of attitudes, but it doesn't stop there. In the real world, love has to grow some skin; it has to become a daily set of behaviors. You need to learn a new set of skills in your relationship, and that will take some time and practice. But if you can develop the right skills, you can experience a great marriage. Do you want me to share those skills with you?"

They looked a little scared, but nodded their heads in agreement. And that's when I showed them what the Bible says about how loving people should treat each other.

There are 59 "one-another" statements in the New Testament. These are the people-skills God is asking every one of us, as His people, to work on. They are behaviors that demonstrate our love. This list is on the longer side, but I encourage you to look it over carefully, because this is what real love looks like.

The 59 "One-Anothers" of the New Testament [8]

1. "...Be at peace with each other." (Mark 9:50)
2. "...Wash one another's feet." (John 13:14)
3. "...Love one another..." (John 13:34)
4. "...Love one another..." (John 13:34)
5. "...Love one another..." (John 13:35)
6. "...Love one another..." (John 15:12)
7. "...Love one another" (John 15:17)
8. "Be devoted to one another in brotherly love..." (Romans 12:10)
9. "...Honor one another above yourselves." (Romans 12:10)
10. "Live in harmony with one another..." (Romans 12:16)
11. "...Love one another..." (Romans 13:8)
12. "...Stop passing judgment on one another." (Romans 14:13)
13. "Accept one another, then, just as Christ accepted you..." (Romans 15:7)
14. "...Instruct one another." (Romans 15:14)
15. "Greet one another with a holy kiss..." (Romans 16:16)
16. "...When you come together to eat, wait for each other." (1 Corinthians 11:33)
17. "...Have equal concern for each other." (1 Corinthians 12:25)
18. "...Greet one another with a holy kiss." (1 Corinthians 16:20)
19. "Greet one another with a holy kiss." (2 Corinthians 13:12)
20. "...Serve one another in love." (Galatians 5:13)

21. "If you keep on biting and devouring each other...you will be destroyed by each other." (Galatians 5:15)
22. "Let us not become conceited, provoking and envying each other." (Galatians 5:26)
23. "Carry each other's burdens..." (Galatians 6:2)
24. "...Be patient, bearing with one another in love." (Ephesians 4:2)
25. "Be kind and compassionate to one another..." (Ephesians 4:32)
26. "...Forgiving each other..." (Ephesians 4:32)
27. "Speak to one another with psalms, hymns, and spiritual songs." (Ephesians 5:19)
28. "Submit to one another out of reverence for Christ." (Ephesians 5:21)
29. "...In humility consider others better than yourselves." (Philippians 2:3)
30. "Do not lie to each other..." (Colossians 3:9)
31. "Bear with each other..." (Colossians 3:13)
32. "...Forgive whatever grievances you may have against one another." (Colossians 3:13)
33. "Teach...[one another]" (Colossians 3:16)
34. "...Admonish one another (Colossians 3:16)
35. "...Make your love increase and overflow for each other." (1 Thessalonians 3:12)
36. "...Love each other." (1 Thessalonians 4:9)
37. "...Encourage each other..."(1 Thessalonians 4:18)
38. "...Encourage each other..." (1 Thessalonians 5:11)
39. "...Build each other up..." (1 Thessalonians 5:11)
40. "Encourage one another daily..." (Hebrews 3:13)
41. "...Spur one another on toward love and good deeds." (Hebrews 10:24)
42. "...Encourage one another." (Hebrews 10:25)
43. "...Do not slander one another." (James 4:11)

44. "Don't grumble against each other..." (James 5:9)
45. "Confess your sins to each other..." (James 5:16)
46. "...Pray for each other." (James 5:16)
47. "...Love one another deeply, from the heart." (1 Peter 3:8)
48. "...Live in harmony with one another..." (1 Peter 3:8)
49. "...Love each other deeply..." (1 Peter 4:8)
50. "Offer hospitality to one another without grumbling." (1 Peter 4:9)
51. "Each one should use whatever gift he has received to serve others..." (1 Peter 4:10)
52. "...Clothe yourselves with humility toward one another..." (1 Peter 5:5)
53. "Greet one another with a kiss of love." (1 Peter 5:14)
54. "...Love one another." (1 John 3:11)
55. "...Love one another." (1 John 3:23)
56. "...Love one another." (1 John 4:7)
57. "...Love one another." (1 John 4:11)
58. "...Love one another." (1 John 4:12)
59. "...Love one another." (2 John 1:5)

Whether it's in the setting of a marriage like Marcus and Cindy's, or on a church ministry team, or a marketplace business group, the rubber really meets the road through our daily behaviors with each other. When we live out these Biblical behaviors, we build a healthy culture of unity, humility, and honor around our lives. This develops much healthier connections, allowing us to become a much healthier team.

Just before we closed our counseling session with prayer together, I encouraged Marcus and Cindy to open their wounded hearts to God's power so that these positive behaviors could become possible in their relationship. "The behaviors of love flow from our hearts and attitudes, not from our heads. None of these behaviors should be forced. Instead, let them be the natural outflows of your daily relationship with Jesus." I could see that something was clicking in them. Hope was rising.

Marcus and Cindy took their copy of the 59 "one-anothers" of the New Testament, and walked out of my office holding hands. We're still in touch, and it has been great to watch how they have learned to put these daily actions to work. They've made their mistakes and hit some bumps along the way, but it's amazing what happens when we follow God's plan for relational health. With every year that passes, I've seen them deepen their commitment to each other and also learn how to meet each other's needs. They are becoming a team and building a healthy relationship together.

THE ART OF HEALTHY RELATIONSHIPS

I have often come back to the shocking honesty of their words that day: Marcus admitting that he was "no good at relationships," and Cindy confessing that she had never experienced a healthy relationship in her life. These problems are heartbreaking, yet all too common. So, I teach on the subject of healthy relationships as often as I can.

I recently asked a group of our high school ministry interns what their experience was with relationships. Our youth ministry does a two-week training intensive for our high school leaders, and I was asked to share something that would help them discover more about leadership. "Let me ask you guys a question. Do you feel like you are good at relationships?" Many of them did, but most admitted that they could do better.

I then explained to them that there is an art to having great relationships. As with music, dance, or drawing, you have to practice and stay with it to get really good. We talked about how beautiful things like good friendships, great marriages, and healthy teams are the result of applying tried and true principles. As leaders in training, we asked ourselves these questions:

- What holds people together?
- What drives us apart?
- How can we build great relationships?

We worked out a list of skills that we thought would be helpful in the art of healthy relationships. Here's what we came up with:

1. Honor everyone

Respect is one of the most important factors in any relationship, and many of the "one-anothers" of the New Testament are about honoring. If we don't place value on others, we won't be able to experience a healthy relationship with them. Jesus said, "Do to others as you would have them do to you" (Luke 6:31). This is still the best way to treat people, no matter who they are or where they are from.

I shared with the kids that day something I learned years ago:

> *Whatever you honor comes toward you*
> *and whatever you dishonor moves further away.*

Nothing pushes people away more than being treated in a dishonoring way. But give someone the honor they deserve, and watch how your relationship will improve. We talked about being careful not to damage our relationships with sarcasm, cynicism, and backbiting. We agreed to be generous with honor and respect, even in the little things like being polite and courteous.

2. Pay attention

Undivided attention is a relational key, and the "one-anothers" of the New Testament imply this kind of focus. Giving someone our attention tells them that they are important to us and to God. It builds their confidence that you care. Even a few minutes of solid attention can help create lifelong bonds between people. The student leaders and I agreed that sometimes we need to put our electronic devices down, face each other, make eye contact, and be sure to have a friendly expression when we communicate.

I'm a task-oriented person, so this is a challenge for me when I'm "on a mission" (as my wife gently reminds me). Too many times, I'll walk right past people I truly love because my mind is on getting something done. I'm learning that part of having healthy relationships and teams is slowing down and paying attention to people. I'm trying to get better at taking my time with others, stopping to say hello to children, and enjoying conversations with young people and those whom others may ignore.

3. Don't be fake

As we talked in the internship meeting, the kids let me know that it really bothers them when people are fake. I think God agrees. Our list of "one-anothers" is not a call to pretend to love, but to genuinely live it out. The apostle Paul said, "Love must be sincere..." (Romans 12:9). And Peter reminds us, "You must show sincere love to each other as brothers and sisters. Love each other deeply with all your heart" (1 Peter 1:22, NLT). Peter chooses the word *anupokritos,* which has been translated as "sincere." It means "without hypocrisy." A "hypocrite" was often an actor who wore a mask. Through Peter's words, God is calling for us to be truly authentic in our relationships.

The English word "sincere" is also illuminating. It comes from the Latin *sine cera,* which means "without wax". In ancient times, vendors hid cracks in their cheap pottery with wax in order to deceive their customers. So honest vendors stamped their wares with the phrase *sine cera*— a promise of authenticity and quality. When it comes to relationships, God is calling us to demonstrate authentic love in a world of fakes and posers—to live without wax in our cracks! God cannot bless who we pretend to be. He can only bless who we really are.

4. Pray together

Part of what makes our internship ministry special is the intentional time our students spend together in prayer. We talked about what a difference this makes in our lives. I remember years ago hearing Dr. Edwin Louis Cole speak at a men's event in our city. He was a great teacher on the subject of relationships. He taught us that husbands, fathers, and friends should pray with the people they love. He explained that prayer has the power to bring us closer in three ways:

- Prayer brings us closer to the One we pray TO.
- Prayer brings us closer to those we pray FOR.
- Prayer brings us closer to those we pray WITH.

As a church staff, we have always made times of prayer together a weekly priority. We step away from our desks and our stacks of important work projects so that we can join our hearts in prayer. I love these times as much as anything I do with our team because prayer is such a great way to connect. Praying together keeps us from coming apart. Whether it's in a marriage, a teenage friendship, a ministry team at church, or a family doing life together, prayer is a powerful way to create lasting relational bonds.

RELATIONAL TEAMS, HEALTHY TEAMS

People need healthy relationships. Human beings are not robots. They are social creatures. They need strong human connections, especially if they're going to do great things together. In fact,

> *Nothing is more crucial to the health of a team than healthy relationships.*

There is an important correlation between team relationships and team health, and until we get relationships right, we'll never get teams right.

Patrick Lencioni has written extensively on organizational health. His book, *The Five Dysfunctions of a Team,* [9] is a classic and perhaps the most insightful resource on the subject of team dynamics available today. In it, Lencioni creates a modern leadership fable that illustrates the basics of teamwork and the perils that must be overcome by every team. As the fable unfolds, five common team dysfunctions are gradually revealed:

- The absence of trust
- Fear in conflict
- Lack of commitment
- Avoidance of accountability, and
- Inattention to results

We'll refer to more of Lencioni's ideas later on in this book, but here is what strikes me as crucial. When I look carefully at these five dysfunctions, it is clear that the majority of them are relational issues: trust, healthy conflict, commitment, and accountability are all things that come up in relationships. If we work alone, we don't have to worry about this list much, but place us on a team and we are "in the tumbler" facing our dysfunctions together.

THE TUMBLER OF TEAMWORK

I will never forget a missions team I was on in Northern India. There were about eight of us traveling around on India's national railroads and local buses to the cities where we were scheduled to do leadership seminars. The Indian people are always amazing, and the culture is fascinating. As expected, the days were long and hot and the accommodations were rough. The unexpected part was the behavior of some on our ministry team.

You would think that experienced pastors and leaders would be mature and patient, but several on the team began pushing for better slots on the speaking schedule, disagreeing over who should lead, and splintering off into angry factions. I thought, *Really?* The stress was building, and one of our speakers had such a severe panic attack that he had to be sedated. I couldn't believe what I was seeing on this team. We were under a full demonic attack, and our relationships were unraveling. We quickly instituted a time for daily prayer together, but for some, it was too little too late. Several of our ministry team members abruptly left the country offended and angry, never to join us again. What a tragedy for our team.

1. In the tumbler, we experience the friction of conflict.

Teams will typically struggle with the same relational issues that couples or families struggle with. Our team of speakers in India was made up of good people, but the heat, conditions, and spiritual warfare created unexpected frictions. When we come together as a team, we should expect to encounter fear, miscommunication, power plays, trust issues, and offenses.

The main point of Steve Job's tumbler story is that relational friction is an inevitable part of the team process. But conflict doesn't have to divide our relationships. If we are smart, conflict can be leveraged as an opportunity to make the team stronger. Friction can refine relationships: "As iron sharpens iron, so one person sharpens another" (Proverbs 27:17, NIV). Just as with that tumbler, our most abrasive interactions can be a part of the process God uses to make us beautiful in the end.

2. In the tumbler, we face the choice to stay or bail.

Have you ever wanted to run from a commitment? The tumbler can tempt us to quit or retreat, just as some on our India speaking team did. One of our staff pastors and his wife recently took some training in healing and spiritual freedom. As a part of the ten-day process, they received hours of prayer and counseling for their personal issues. He confessed that it was, at times, a brutal process. After the first five or six days, he and his wife were making good progress but grew weary and tempted to leave early. "We've been blessed, but this is exhausting," they mused. "Perhaps a few days of rest instead of finishing the entire seminar would be better." They decided to stay and finish, and the breakthroughs continued until the work God was doing in them was complete. The temptation to bail from the tumbler of the team can be strong, but enduring to the end pays big dividends.

3. In the tumbler, we sharpen our people skills.

There is nothing like the laboratory of real relationships to test our relational skills. Listening to sermons, reading books, and getting counseling can all help us collect the principles we need to build healthy relationships, marriages, and teams. However, there is no substitute for real life in the tumbler. The collisions begin after we say, "I do," and then join the team. This is when we are able to put our theories into practice and we discover what works and what doesn't work in relationships. God is teaching us in the tumbler, and it is vital.

The conflicts we experienced in India were the magnifying glass of God revealing the gaps in our relational skills and heart attitudes. He was showing us our need to communicate, honor, trust, and work together. In the tumbler of the team, if we will focus on love and put our "one-anothers" into practice, we'll grow closer with each rotation of the coffee can.

4. In the tumbler, we get polished and become beautiful.

Kathy and I spent our early years in Christ experiencing the beauty of close relationships. The Jesus movement of the early 1970s was touching scores of young people in our nation, especially on the West Coast, and our small church was experiencing genuine renewal and revival. We didn't have large programs or great facilities, but we had heavenly worship, passionate prayer meetings, and a growing influence. We were a spiritual family, filled with real love, fervent devotion, and a unique bond with each other.

As time marched on, however, some of our relationships became strained. I can remember offenses, suspicions, and resentments arising here and there. At times, though, it felt like there were waves of spiritual attacks on relationships. Relational breakdowns seemed to be spreading, and larger groups of people were being affected. People questioned our culture, our leaders, and our beliefs. Over time, more than a few people left our small church, while others stayed. We were in the tumbler off and on for several years, and it was a painful time marked by loss and separation. Many wondered how this could be happening to such a close group of people.

The years came and went. People got married, moved to other cities, started businesses, and pursued their dreams. Our church slowly came out of the turbulence and has emerged much stronger. We now have better programs and facilities, and hopefully we have retained the markers of spiritual passion and great relationships that we knew in the early 70s. Still, there has been a lingering question in many of our minds: why did all that happen? How could we lose so many relationships and that special sense of community we all shared together?

Recently, someone decided to have a reunion for everyone who had been a part of our church in those days. The invites went out over social media, and nearly a hundred of us from all over California made plans to get to the gathering. I'm sure we all wondered how it would all go. Could we recapture some of the closeness that we had enjoyed forty years before, or was it too late? Would old wounds open up and grow worse?

We gathered at Seacliff State Beach in Aptos on a perfect summer day to share food, exchange memories, and have a good time. The relational chemistry was instant. People were hugging, laughing, and sharing photographs of the old days. Guitars came out, and we sang the songs we'd sung in church together forty years before. The presence of the Lord dropped down on everyone, just as it had so many times in the early days. We were back in close connection, and it seemed as though no time had passed.

Later on that day, as the sun was setting, the speeches began. One by one, those who had been through that season in the tumbler celebrated their personal memories. Person after person remarked about how precious our connections were and how much we had added to each other's faith and love for God. The tears flowed, the old issues were put into perspective, and the flow of healing was intense.

Forty years later, we were in agreement about what really mattered: life was all about relationships. We were rich—richer than we ever dreamed—because we still had each other. The friction of the tumbler had not broken our team apart. It had actually polished and revealed the beauty of our relationships.

Life is all about the loving connections that God gives us. Healthy relationships are held together by love and a set of corresponding behaviors. When it comes to healthy teams, we must have healthy relationships marked by these same healthy behaviors. Friction is an inevitable part of relationships, whether it is in a marriage, friendships, our work life, or a church ministry team. But if we will stay in the tumbler, over time God will smooth out our rough spots and unlock the beauty of our relationships.

Conversation #2

TALK IT OVER

After you've read the Chapter on THE BEAUTY OF RELATIONSHIPS, take a few minutes with your group to talk through some of the questions below. Give everyone a chance to share, and encourage everyone to be honest, authentic, and supportive of others. Always remember to affirm vulnerability and thank those who are willing to share and ask for prayer.

1. I love Rev. Dick Foth's definition of what how love looks in action: "Love is the accurate estimation and adequate supply of another person's need" (page 32). What skills are required to accurately estimate someone else's need? What character traits must we possess in order to truly become adequate suppliers of the needs of others?

2. With so many competing priorities and tasks clamoring for our attention, how can we possibly find the time to make love our highest goal as Paul commands? What practical strategies toward this end can you come up with?

3. Based on the list of Scriptures on pages 5 and 6, it is clear God is very interested in our relationships and how we treat one another, and yet we live in a very self-focused culture. What are some of the tangible things we can do to live counter-culturally and fulfill these Scriptures?

4. One of the Five Dysfunctions of a Team that Patrick Lencioni writes about is Fear of Conflict. Most of us try to avoid conflict whenever possible, but in order for a team to work well, healthy conflict is actually essential. How can conflict "be an opportunity to make a team stronger" (page 43)? What are some of the differences between healthy conflict and conflict that is destructive?

5. When we are in the tumbler of real relationships, our first instinct is often to get out. Having our rough edges smoothed out by rubbing against others hurts! "The temptation to bail from the tumbler of the team can be strong, but enduring to the end pays big dividends (page 43)." Think about your experiences of sticking it out in the tumbler. What are some of these dividends?

6. Many people can identify with the story of Marcus and Cindy. Perhaps you are one of them. You don't think you are good at relationships because you have never experienced relationships that are truly healthy. Marcus and Cindy were encouraged by the hope that things could get better, so they trusted their counselor and began to work very hard on their relationship. How important is hope to succeeding in relationships? What must we do in order to receive hope and impart hope to others?

7. I conclude the leadership take-away with saying "forgive yourself for falling short" (page 51). If you are a leader who sincerely wants to become better, reading a book like this can feel like holding a huge magnifying glass on your mistakes and shortcomings. You are not alone! Every good leader has felt like a failure at one point or another. Take some time and share with your group an area where you have fallen short and need to forgive yourself.

Conversation #2

TEAM UP AND MAKE IT BETTER

Before you end your group conversation...

- Think about someone in your life—perhaps someone on your team—that you'd like to have a better relationship with. Consider reaching out to them, blessing them in some way, or apologizing if needed. What is the first step you might take toward a better relationship? Do it today.

- Prayer is one of our most powerful relationship tools. Review on [page 8] the three ways prayer brings us closer. How does being drawn closer to God help us in our earthly relationships? How do you feel when someone says they are praying for you? How about when they take the time to pray with you?

- Practice this principle of prayer right now. Start by thanking the Lord for His forgiveness and forgiving yourself for the shortcomings shared from #7 under *Talk It Over.* Then pray for each other, believing together for the Lord to bring growth in these areas.

Sometime before your next conversation...

- Review this chapter and note anything that you've decided to change in your life. Talk to God about it, and make a decision to get started by faith.

- Read the next chapter so you'll be ready to have a great conversation when your group gets together next.

LEADERSHIP TAKE-AWAY #2:

"Healthy Leaders Cultivate
Healthy Team Relationships"

If you are leading a family, group or ministry, you are so important to God. You have massive potential to bless the world. He wants all kinds of fruitfulness to be alive in you. But for that to happen, you have to get connected and functioning in relationships. You have a really hard job, and at times you will surely find yourself in the tumbler. Just remember: the relationships you cultivate become the basis of your success as a leader.

See yourself as a gardener, cultivating the relationships on your team. As you do this, keep these simple leadership tips in mind:

- *Make love your greatest goal.* Great leaders lead because they love. It is the quality of our connections that determines the level of our influence. A leader that loves people will never be irrelevant. Love is a leader's North Star—without keeping it in view, we'll get lost in busyness, pressure, and fatigue. "Live a life filled with love, following the example of Christ. He loved us and offered himself as a sacrifice for us..." (Ephesians 5:2, NLT). Without loving, healthy relationships, a leader will struggle to have healthy teams, so spend time with your team. Get to really know them. Love on them and let authentic affection be the centerpiece of your leadership culture.

- *Let love be your main message.* Teach people about healthy relationships. They want to hear your voice. There are surprisingly few books written for leaders about love. Books on vision, strategy, organization, and communication abound, but why aren't we more focused on learning to truly love the people we lead? Both Alexander Strauch and Perry Noble have helped us with this need, writing leadership books based on love. [10] Dig deep into the topic and return to it often. Relationships are your greatest leadership currency, so buy it up and sell it often: "No matter what I say, what I believe, and what I do, I'm bankrupt without love" (1 Corinthians 13:3, MSG).

- *Practice the little things that make love real.* Walk more slowly around people. Work on being present and giving people attention with authentic conversations. Take the mask off and be real. Listen and learn from others. Help them work through the friction that they are experiencing with other team members. Be generous with honor and encouragement. Give your team members the spotlight, and praise their successes openly. Be honest when they need to do better, but do it privately. Show a genuine interest in their personal lives, especially the new ones and the younger ones. Ask them about their families, their jobs, and their daily struggles. Share some of your own, and pray with your team on a regular basis.

- *Fight daily for your relationships.* As a leader, you know that the enemy is constantly resisting you. He wants nothing more than to weaken and rob you of your relationships. He knows how powerfully relationships determine your leadership potential. What greater victory could he achieve than to introduce division, separation, and isolation on your team? I am proud of how you courageously face this fight every day. Don't get weary in the battle. Rest, draw near to the Lord, gather your intercessors, and stay strong in the fight. Be a watchman over your family and team relationships, and as Nehemiah said, "fight for your families, your sons and your daughters, your wives and your homes" (Nehemiah 4:14, NIV).

- *Forgive yourself for falling short.* If you are like me, you've made plenty of mistakes with people. You may have put tasks and rules ahead of relationships. You may have been too demanding or distant. Sometimes we as leaders fail to see life through the eyes of our followers. We move too fast, and fail to be sensitive to people's needs, desires, and perspectives. Listen to what God is teaching you, and keep growing. As you do this, be gentle with yourself. God has not given up on you, and He will use your life even though you are imperfect. God used

Abraham, who was prone to lying, Moses who struggled with anger, David who sinned, and Peter who sometimes leaped before he looked. Stay in the tumbler; you are just beginning to shine!

THERE'S NO TEAM WITHOUT TRUST

"A team is not a group of people who work together.
A team is a group of people who trust each other."
— SIMON SINEK

Seattle businessman Don Bennett was on top of the world—wealthy, successful in business, loved by his family and blessed with good health. Then, on a sunny day in August of 1972, everything changed. Don was boating with his children when he suddenly fell overboard. The spinning blades of the propeller sliced through his legs, and he nearly bled to death. Before it was over, Don Bennett's left leg needed 480 stitches and his right leg was completely gone from the knee down.

Don's challenges were just beginning. During his long hospitalization, he lost his business. He felt as if he had nothing left in life—except his remarkable tenacity. Don went to work and taught himself to ski again and then took up kayaking. After he had built another successful business, he began to dream of something many would call crazy: he wanted to return to mountain climbing.

Don had climbed Mt. Rainer in 1970, and he was now determined to do it again. He knew he couldn't do it without help, so he assembled a team he could trust—four others who could help him achieve his seemingly impossible dream. After a period of rigorous preparation, his team felt that he had the ability he needed to press past his physical limitations. Don trusted his team, and together they returned to the mountain. He climbed for five days, 14 hours a day, often struggling with his crutches and even crawling face down. On July 15, 1982, ten years after his devastating injury, Don

Bennett reached the summit at 14,410 feet to become the first amputee to climb Mt. Rainer.

When asked about the most important lesson he learned during his ordeal, his response was simple: "You can't do it on your own." [11] For Don, it was all about having a team he could trust.

TRUST IS THE FOUNDATION

Trust has long been championed by many of the world's leading voices as the key to team success. In Patrick Lencioni's *The Five Dysfunctions of a Team*, he asserts that trust is the foundation of a great team. To drive this point home, Lencioni pictures healthy teamwork as a five layered pyramid, the first layer of which is trust. A strong foundation of trust holds everything else in place, and without it, every other team advantage will invariably collapse.

In *Team of Teams*, retired General Stanley McChrystal challenges organizations to build healthy teams just as he did in the fight to defeat Al Qaeda. For McChrystal, a team's ability to trust is central to victory. He emphasizes the secret of elite Navy SEAL teams, stating, "The purpose of BUD/S (Basic Underwater Demolition/SEAL) is not to build super soldiers. It is to build superteams. The first step of this is constructing a strong lattice of *trusting relationships.*" [12]

A few years back, here in Silicon Valley, Google did a massive study on team performance. It confirmed that the best teams have one thing in common: a sense of safety. Paul Santagata, Head of Industry at Google said it best: "There's no team without trust." [13]

Trust is a firm belief in the reliability of something. When you trust your team, you believe that they are reliable, capable, and unlikely to fail you. Some years ago, a group of our young adults decided to go skydiving, and they invited Kathy and I to join them. Because Kathy is sane, she declined, but of course I agreed to go along and pay $200 to jump out of a perfectly good airplane. As I listened to the instructions I was given before the jump, I felt confident in the team of professional instructors with whom we were jumping. I believed they understood this process well and would not fail us. We strapped on our equipment together and boarded the plane with our instructors. So far, so good.

But when we got to the proper altitude, and the countdown began, it was time to really see if we trusted our jump instructors. If we jumped, it would only be because we trusted our team. One by one, as each of us glided safely toward the earth, we knew we had accomplished something special together that would not have been possible apart from trust.

TRUST IS THE WAY TO THE TOP

Mountain climbers like Don Bennett are a great example of the importance of trust and teamwork. They know that to get to the top of any mountain, you need to have a closely connected team pulling with you.

If great teams are like mountain climbers, what is the key to getting to the top together? Again, the answer is trust. Trust has the ability to empower people to go to places together that they could never get to by themselves.

In the spring of 1953, two mountain climbers became the first men in history to reach the top of Mt. Everest. Edmund Hillary was a beekeeper from New Zealand, and his trusted Nepalese Sherpa was named Tenzing Norgay. Together, they made the brutal journey to the previously untouched top of the world—a 29,000-foot frozen peak.

On their descent afterwards, Hillary slipped and began to fall. Fearing certain death, Hillary was relieved when Norgay drove his ice axe into solid ground and held onto the rope which linked them together. Hillary's life was spared because of this heroic action. In subsequent media interviews, Norgay remained calm and dismissive of any praise for him personally. To those who shouted questions, he simply felt that this kind of partnership and trust were basic, saying, "Mountain climbers always help each other." [14]

The late Billy Graham made it to the top of another kind of mountain, perhaps one that is more significant. He was undoubtedly the most respected evangelist the world has ever known. How did he get to the top of his dream to reach the world? Graham is famous for building a ministry team that stayed with him throughout his long ministry, helping him to reach an estimated 200 million souls for Christ. Both George Beverly Shea, Graham's soloist, and Cliff Barrows, Graham's Music Director, served on this team for nearly 60 years.

After Graham's death in February of 2018, another long-time member of his team, Art Bailey, described Graham's unique ability as a team builder who trusted others: "...He had gifts that were integral to what we did and so did others," Bailey said, "and he trusted them, and that served us well these last 60 years." [15]

The greatest evangelist in modern history created a team that was held together by strong ropes of personal trust. His team took him to the top of his ministry potential, and it will do the same for you.

MOVING TO THE NEXT LEVEL

There are two broad levels of trust that any team can experience. The first level helps us function, but only the second will cause us to flourish.

Assumed Trust is where we assume we can generally trust something or someone. For example, if you are sitting as you read this, you are assuming you can trust your chair to hold your weight and not collapse. Or imagine, perhaps, that you are vacationing with some friends. You assume you can trust the pilots and the airline to get all of you to your destination safely. Having landed in a city you've never been to before, you are all excited. You walk to the escalator that leads you to an elevator, trusting both to get you to the car rental counter. You rent a car together, load your luggage into the car, and drive toward your hotel, all the while assuming that the drivers in oncoming lanes of traffic will not cross the yellow lines and hit you. In fact, danger barely crosses your mind during the journey.

This is a level of trust that is basic to functioning in life. Though you and your friends have never met the pilots, the mechanics at the car rental agency, or the drivers you pass along the way, everything works out well enough. You know that if you want to get to your hotel and relax, you must make reasonable assumptions about the behavior and abilities of others. Assumed trust is generally adequate to get us where we're going, but when it comes to building a healthy team, it's not enough.

Achieved Trust is a much stronger level of trust. It is based on a personal relationship or a personal experience that tells us, "These guys would never let me down—I know them." We achieve this level of trust when we have functioned smoothly together over time. We trust in this way because we have direct experience with each other's character. We've been vulnerable, withstood conflict, and lived through setbacks, all without losing that sense of faithfulness and commitment toward each another.

Achieved trust is the level of trust that empowers us to flourish. Let's return to our example of vacationing with friends. Having arrived at your hotel, everyone gets cleaned up and goes out to enjoy a meal together. As the food is served and the conversation unfolds, one of your friends makes an insensitive remark that injures several at the table. Instantly, the mood changes. What had been laughter becomes awkward silence. What had been the anticipation of shared pleasure now degenerates to doubt: *Is this vacation going to end badly? We've paid all this money and come all this way, and now what?*

The tension builds, but then, somewhere deep down, the group's collective memory kicks in. One by one, you come back to everything you have experienced together as a group. You have a team memory—an instinct deep inside that reassures you that this momentary setback can and will be resolved.

One of you offers words of healing and perspective. Others second the motion, and the mood at the table quickly becomes supportive and conciliatory again. Your friend apologizes, and then, to everyone's surprise, explains that she has recently become anxious and upset because of the concerning results of a medical test. Now everyone completely forgets the offense and bands together to support the one they've loved for so long. Tears flow, hugs are shared, and the group becomes stronger. The vacation is an unforgettable triumph. It has strengthened the bonds of trust and love in each person's heart. The friendships deepen rather than fracture because the group has moved to the next level of trust.

WHAT DOES TEAM TRUST LOOK LIKE?

In my time as a Lead Pastor of a growing church, I have had a chance to experience trust with a lot of teams. I lead our executive team as we work together on policy and direction. I lead a preaching team that creates the Sunday content for all of our campuses. I sit on a creative culture team that works together on music, decor, branding, atmospheres for events, and much more. Our list of teams goes on, as many of these teams are composed of the leaders of other teams. We have become a church building upon a "team of teams" concept. Nearly everything I do in ministry involves teamwork on one level or another because we believe teams are the right way to do things, and they bring so many advantages to a church. That's what this book is all about.

The people on my team are strong, bright, and experienced. Our teams are diverse in background, perspective, and gifting. We often see things very differently, but I really look forward to our times together because we have the kind of trust in our team that enables us to flourish.

When there is trust on a team, everyone feels safe and confident, even if things aren't perfectly smooth. High levels of team trust enable everyone to be less anxious about how the team will get along and perform. When there is trust, a team communicates well. Conflicts can become constructive rather than destructive, and great decisions get made. Most importantly, when disappointments or changes arise, the team can bounce back because it has been built on a strong foundation.

> *When a team is filled with trust, it is*
> *freed to flourish in its potential.*

What happens when there is a lack of trust on a team? Years ago one of the young leaders in our church began to struggle with the people he was leading. Kenneth was bright and full of creative ideas. He knew the Bible and loved our church, but he had a forceful personality and frequently came on too strong with people. I began to hear reports from those who worked with him. At first, they were subtle: "Kenneth is a really intense leader, isn't he?" or "Wow, that guy has a big personality!"

As time went on, however, the volume grew louder as more of his character flaws began to rub people raw. Kenneth was known to exaggerate and oversell. He often overstepped personal boundaries with people, and at times he said things about his team members that a leader should not say. Trust was breaking down on Kenneth's team.

I knew what these team members were feeling because I had experienced a similar breakdown of trust years before when I had just entered into ministry. George was my supervisor, and he taught me the hard way that a leader who doesn't trust his team can make them quite miserable. George was suspicious of everyone on the team. He stood over our workspaces several times a day, asking "Whatcha doing?" He kept written lists of infractions and often reminded us of our shortcomings. He fined people nickels for breaking the rules and one time actually directed me to turn my desk away from a scenic window and toward a blank wall because I'd be less tempted to daydream facing the wall! I really hated working on a team where there was so little trust.

59

*The problem with a lack of trust on a team is that
it undermines the team's morale and commitment.*

When there is no trust, people are resentful, defensive, and
unmotivated. Selfish agendas develop. People begin to jockey for
position, trying climb over the heads of those they see as
competitors. Because team members don't feel safe, they undermine
authority, hoarding information and setting up social cliques to
protect themselves. All of this leads to an unhealthy morale, bad
decisions, wasted energy, and damage to people's lives.

This is what I saw developing on Kenneth's team. When good
people started stepping off his team, I realized it was past time for us
to talk about the true nature of leadership and taking care of people,
as well as the importance of cultivating trust on a team.

FOUR ANCHORS OF TEAM TRUST

Kenneth and I started to meet regularly to discuss how things were
going on his team and what could be done to turn things around. It
was a really difficult series of conversations for several reasons. By
nature, I don't enjoy correcting people I care about. I love Kenneth,
but it was clear he needed my correction. Also, I knew Kenneth's
communication style could be defensive, evasive, and blaming when
he was under pressure. I never knew what he was going to say next,
and it felt like this might be a mess.

I was facing a mountain of mixed emotions—part of me wanting to
replace Kenneth for the sake of his team, and another part of me
fighting to see him grow and preserve his future as a leader. I knew
something had to be done, so by faith I pushed ahead into the
journey.

Our discussions centered around four principles for building trust
on a team. I like to look at these four ideas as analogous to the
anchors that mountain climbers rely on when they are climbing—
the small devices they use to secure themselves to their climbing
surface. These "anchors of team trust" will secure us as we work

our way to the top of the challenge of building healthy teams. Without them, we will surely slip and fall, but using them wisely allows us to ascend to new heights together.

Anchor #1 - *Credibility in Team Leadership*

We started with the role of a leader in fostering team trust. "Kenneth, every team has to have a leader that is credible. By that, I mean people need to believe you are safe, reliable, and always thinking of their good. The problem on your team is that you are undermining that sense of trust by the way you relate to people and communicate." Kenneth shifted uncomfortably in his seat, but I saw potential in him as a leader, so I shared what I understood about credibility in a leader's life.

In the Gospels, we see that Jesus had the quality of credibility. Thousands trusted Him and felt safe in His presence. This was especially true of His team; the closer they got to Jesus, the more convinced of His message they became. Everyone who saw his miracles and heard his teachings understood that Jesus was unlike any other leader. They followed Him because He spoke with uncommon authority and love (see Luke 4:32).

Credibility in leadership is first and foremost about rock-solid character. In 1 Timothy 1 and Titus 3, God's qualifications for leaders are listed. The majority of these requirements are character-based as opposed to ability-based. Several ability-based requirements are given, such as the ability to teach or the ability to manage one's home affairs. But when it comes to character, the list really expands. God highlights the contours of true leadership with the brushstrokes of self-control, wisdom, respectability, gentleness, and devotion. Leaders must not be drunkards, fighters, hot heads, controllers, or spiritual children. In other words,

Leadership is about character and credibility.

Credibility and leadership are two sides of the same coin. Place an unreliable leader into a position of authority, and everything breaks down. But when a leader is trusted, a team can flourish:

> "Remove impurities from the silver and the silversmith can craft a fine chalice; Remove the wicked from leadership and authority will be credible and God-honoring."
> PROVERBS 25:4-5 MSG

When leaders are not credible, they have lost their ability to lead and influence their team. As I explained to Kenneth, once that happens, there is nothing that anyone can do to prevent a leader from losing his or her team. If you lose credibility, you lose influence. If you lose influence, you lose your team.

The importance of this kind of credibility in a leader's life became painfully clear to me years ago when I was asked to assist a group of pastors in dealing with Carl, their overseer. These pastors and leaders reluctantly told me how they had come to see Carl as dishonest. At the time, Carl was a rising star in some ministry circles, but his closest associates were growing more and more frustrated with what they saw as real character and credibility issues.

For example, when speaking at conferences, Carl would tell glowing stories of his military experiences. Unfortunately, his team began to notice timeline problems and other inconsistencies in his stories. Though they loved Carl and hoped that they were mistaken, suspicions compounded with each new telling of the story. When gently confronted, Carl defended his tall tales, claiming they were accurate. Reluctantly, Carl's team fact-checked his military record and found evidence that his claims were impossible.

There were other issues as well. Carl commonly spoke of his brief career in professional sports before an injury derailed him, as well as a public confrontation with a politician, both stories designed to give him an aspect of heroism. Sadly, these stories were also checked and found to be fictional. When they confronted Carl with everything, they did it with strength and love.

Under pressure, Carl admitted a few errors in judgment, and

quickly asked for everyone's understanding and support. But the admissions were too shallow, and the damage to Carl's credibility had gone too deep. One of the hardest things any of us will ever do is to trust after our trust has been broken. Before it was over, Carl's credibility and team trust were gone, and the network that he led imploded.

Anchor #2 - *Integrity in Team Character*

Kenneth was listening, but at times he felt the need to point out that he was not the only one at fault. One by one, he referenced the many character flaws in his team members, citing examples of their immaturity, missteps, and refusal to follow his direction. My pulse quickened because I have little patience for leaders who blame their team. At the same time, I understood that team trust is not just about good leadership—it's about each member of the team being trustworthy as well.

The second anchor of trust on a team relates to the character of the team members—and specifically the character quality of integrity. When you are climbing together, you need to know that your partner will not flake out on you. When team members have integrity, others can feel safe in trusting them, but without personal integrity in each member of the team, the team cannot trust. Each of us needs to be a faithful and reliable member of the team. When we understand God and who He calls us to be, we realize that,

Who we are is more important to God than what we do.

What is integrity? Integrity is having a morally undivided heart. It is the unbroken connection between our convictions and our conduct. When the link between our beliefs and our character becomes disconnected, they are no longer *integrated*—and thus we lack integrity. When our integrity is broken, we will struggle to be faithful, reliable, and fruitful.

Nothing that remains deeply fractured can carry God's presence or purpose. This is one reason why Jesus demanded integrity in the

63

life of everyone who follows Him:

> "Let your light so shine before men that they may see your
> moral excellence and your praiseworthy, noble, and good
> deeds and recognize and honor and praise and glorify your
> Father Who is in heaven." MATTHEW 5:16 AMP

> "Don't say anything you don't mean...You only make things
> worse when you lay down a smoke screen of pious talk,
> saying, 'I'll pray for you,' and never doing it, or saying, 'God
> be with you,' and not meaning it. You don't make your
> words true by embellishing them with religious lace. In
> making your speech sound more religious, it becomes less
> true. Just say 'yes' and 'no.' When you manipulate words to
> get your own way, you go wrong."
> MATTHEW 5:33-37 MSG

The one thing I wanted Kenneth to understand more than anything
was the vital relationship between integrity and team trust.
"Kenneth, as a leader, your integrity is where it all begins. If you
have integrity, your team will follow you faithfully, because they
will trust you. The level of integrity will rise on the entire team,
and with it, team trust will increase."

I had discovered this anchor years before as I studied the nature of
influence. Why do people follow leaders? What is the secret to
being a leader people can trust? I found out that integrity and
character were the common denominators in every successful
leader's life. I am convinced of this:

Integrity is the most powerful currency of influence.

Edward R. Murrow is considered one of journalism's greatest
figures. He was noted for honesty and integrity in delivering the
news. He is reported to have once said, "To be persuasive, we must
be believable. To be believable, we must be credible. To be credible,
we must be truthful." I believe he understood something essential
about integrity.

"Kenneth, when you exaggerate and oversell, you are destroying your team's trust in you. When you make a promise and then dismiss their disappointment when you don't deliver, you are damaging them and their support for you. They feel free to dismiss your direction and become unreliable workers because you are not reliable. I know they are not perfect, but you are responsible to inspire and influence them. Don't blame them for their issues; lead them to a better place."

I reminded Kenneth that if he would demonstrate integrity in word and action, his team would quickly follow his lead. David, the greatest leader in ancient Israel, was able to build a legendary team of loyal warriors from a collection of dropouts and malcontents (see 1 Samuel 22:2). He was certainly a gifted man, but charisma alone doesn't carry a leader to success. David was able to form a world-class team out of average followers because of his character. David was the kind of leader who would vow, "I will pay attention to the way of integrity...I will live with a heart of integrity in my house." (Psalm 101:2, HCSB). Those closest to him would have seen this, and been inspired to rise above their own shortcomings.

Kenneth looked at his shoes, and I could tell he felt badly, so I assured him that he didn't have to be perfect—no one does. "Keep in mind that integrity does not mean perfection. David was a flawed man and he failed God miserably at times. All of us fail and make mistakes in leadership. You can certainly see how that's true of me, since we work closely together. There is no such thing as a perfect leader, Kenneth. Yet when we value integrity, we are setting the pace for our team."

Anchor #3 - *Clarity in Team Culture*

Over the course of our talks together, Kenneth and I also agreed that his team lacked clarity, and I had a part to play in that regard. At that time, there had been some confusion with changes we were making in several areas of our church, and this was affecting Kenneth's team through no fault of his own. Some of his efforts to build his team were falling short with people because they were filtering everything through their feelings and experiences with larger issues in the church.

I took responsibility for my role in that, admitting we needed an infusion of clarity across our growing ministries. Without intending to, we had been moving too fast and making too many changes. We failed to make sure people understood why we were changing things and how things would look in the future, and this contributed to a feeling of lost trust in some parts of the church, including Kenneth's areas.

Patrick Lencioni has a lot to say about the importance of clarity. In *The Advantage: Why Organizational Health Trumps Everything Else in Business,* [16] Lencioni champions four "disciplines" any team has to have in order to be healthy. Three of the four centers on clarity—creating clarity, over-communicating clarity, and reinforcing clarity.

For Lencioni, building a healthy team means making sure everyone on the team clearly understands why the team exists, what makes the team unique, what is the most important thing the team should be doing right now, and where the team is heading in the future. Through constant reinforcement of these ideas, we avoid the loss of team trust.

An atmosphere of clarity encourages the team to flourish.

Some of Kenneth's struggles with his team were being mirrored elsewhere in the church. So what did we do to fix this? Following Lencioni's advice, we took the time to make sure our top leaders had clarity. We had meetings—lots of meetings! One-on-ones, department meetings, staff meetings, and campus leadership meetings. We talked, answered questions, taught, and listened for months. I gathered our elders, admitted my missteps in moving too fast, and asked everyone to forgive me. It took some time, but as we communicated and were honest, clarity and trust were simultaneously restored, and our team began to move forward together again.

Clarity in culture is especially important to the team. A culture is the atmosphere that surrounds the team; it is a system of beliefs, values, behaviors, and practices. It is what gives a team or a church its own unique feel and presence. Every team has a culture. The big question is: Is it creating trust? This is where Kenneth and I returned to his style of leadership and how it was affecting his team.

"Some cultures are healthy and life-giving while others are toxic and dysfunctional. What we are facing with your team is a culture of mistrust and resentment. Let's turn this around and create a great team culture," I exhorted. "Great team cultures attract great team members, while unhealthy cultures repel them. If we can build a clear and attractive team culture, your people will accomplish incredible things, your team will grow, and you'll love leading them."

Our next steps involved getting clarity back into Kenneth's team. To create a clear team culture, we needed to deal with specific questions like,

- Who are we?
- What do we do?
- How do we do it?
- What does a "win" look like for us?

Taking a page from our recent church playbook, Kenneth started setting up his own meetings to turn things around. He knew it would take time, and it did, but eventually his team got to a better place.

While he was working on clarity in his team culture, I saw another team in our church that needed clarity. Some time later, I took our worship team leaders through a series of conversations over a six-month period of time. We met monthly to re-imagine our worship team's culture. We discussed styles, opinions, attitudes, current trends, and team requirements. We talked about "culture killers" and "culture builders," as well as our unique worship culture based on Scripture, our history, and especially our vision of what's ahead.

Every month, the discussion was lively as people became engaged and unified in what we saw as the right direction for our worship team's culture. When it was all done, we had written a manual called *GateWay's Worship Culture* [17] that is now a tool for creating and reinforcing clarity with existing and new musicians and team members.

There is nothing more powerful than creating clarity in a team's culture. Clarity has been like an extra shot of espresso to our entire church, boosting our culture to a new level of energy and confidence. This third anchor of team trust unites, refines, and brings direction to everything. But there is one final anchor that ultimately secures team trust.

Anchor 4 - *Candor in Team Communication*

One of the most toxic dynamics that was brewing on Kenneth's team was in the area of communication. There were so many mixed messages and misunderstandings that people were quickly losing trust. I have come to believe that 90% of our relational problems are simple miscommunications made worse by overreactions, and this was proving to be the case on Kenneth's team.

As the reports of trouble increased, I saw that there was also a supernatural attack affecting communication on his team. It made my stomach turn when I discerned that a "spirit of separation" [18] was succeeding in breaking relationships through offense and misunderstanding. The enemy takes natural issues and seeks to create supernatural problems, so it can get complicated. For the purposes of this anchor of trust, let's focus on the natural side of team communication.

Effective teams are made up of people who are eager to talk straight with each other. Open, straightforward communication is crucial to an atmosphere of trust, as thought-leaders like Lencioni frequently emphasize. Even though the prospect of candor and robust dialogue in the team setting can seem scary to many of us, teams need to feel the freedom to be candid with each other if they are going to be healthy. [19]

If your team is afraid to "tell it like it is,"
you have a team communication issue.

One of my favorite teams is our church's creative team. We spend a
lot of time designing the look and feel of our music, facility, and
ministry events, and this requires us to face our fears about talking
straight with each other. Creative people rarely see things the same
way, and they can have strong feelings when it comes to aesthetics
and personal taste.

Human beings by nature can be sensitive about our ideas and
thoughts, and that includes me. We can fall prey to the temptation
of keeping things surface in communication so as not to "rock the
boat." Agreement is truly important, as we'll see in the next
chapter, but when we are tempted to agree with everyone's ideas,
good or bad, just to keep the peace and avoid hurting each other, we
can't win as a team. The fear of honesty prevents us from truly
collaborating to create amazing ideas. When we strictly aim to
"keep the peace" in communication, everyone feels bridled,
creativity is squelched and the end result is unremarkable.

To draw out our creative team's best, I try to encourage robust
dialogue, even when it means disagreement: "We all have our
opinions, and an opinion is not right or wrong," I'll remind them.
"It is vital that everyone here share without fear and without getting
too sensitive. Today we may not see the issues the same way, but
together we are going to make great decisions, so speak your mind
and let's honor everyone's perspective."

I'm happy to say that we are growing in candor and no one has
died! Our creative team is growing stronger and more creative
because we are raising our trust levels and lowering our fears of
robust communication. We are not afraid to candidly say, "I don't
love that idea..." and still be a team. This also applies to my ideas.
As I allow my suggestions to be challenged—sometimes painfully
so— we make much better decisions, and we have a much better

team. You see,

People have more "buy in" when they
are given a chance to "weigh in."

Part of what was complicating things on Kenneth's team was the
fear some people had of communicating their concerns back to a
leader who was in authority. If people believe that because you are
in charge, you cannot be questioned or challenged when things
aren't clear, that's a problem. I found that there were many who
wanted to say something about Kenneth's leadership style, but who
were being "good soldiers."

I appreciate respect and honor, but was alarmed when I spoke to
different members of Kenneth's team who had held back too long. I
reminded them, "If you notice a problem, that doesn't make you
the problem. Being straight when you are communicating is a trust-
builder on a team, so send clear signals. Be humble, but ask lots of
questions and pull out of your leaders and fellow team members
what you need from them. Then clarify what you are hearing to be
sure it is accurate."

In creating a culture of team candor, we need wisdom. It can be
risky to share the truth with someone you don't fully trust. We
should ask ourselves, how appropriate is my honesty, given my
current level of relationship with this person?

We should also remember that being honest is good, but being
ruthlessly honest is cruel. Consider the hearts of your team
members as you "speak the truth in love" (Ephesians 4:15). The
goal is to *build* the team, not dismantle it—to encourage team
members, not discourage them. If there are differences of opinion,
affirm one another personally as you disagree. Warm tones and
respectful words in times of conflict signal to others that the
relationship is not at risk. Using healthy methods of communication
will contribute to growing trust on the team.

As Kenneth and I worked our way through his personal and team issues, everything was starting to add up. We were discovering together how each missing anchor in Kenneth's ministry was exposing him to the weight of mistrust all around him. What had felt mysterious now made perfect sense: a forceful personality, the gaps in his character, and unhealthy personal and spiritual dynamics were keeping his team from achieving trust and moving to the top. Throw in the weight of communication breakdowns and a toxic atmosphere of change and anxiety, and it was easy to see why Kenneth and his team were pinned down, scared, and stuck on the side of a mountain, feeling like there was no place to go.

As we talked through the four anchors of team trust, the mountain still looked big, but we knew it was no longer impossible to climb. Kenneth and I overcame our fears, tethered our hearts, and committed to climbing together.

Over the coming months, we stayed connected and helped each other like good mountain climbers do. We took personal responsibility where we needed to, and encouraged everyone on Kenneth's team to do the same. We talked honestly with his team, apologized one-by-one, and made peace where we could. Listening to each member of the team was an important part of moving to the next level. Remember, you can't do it alone. You have to trust your team.

Not everyone stayed on the team, and a few were wounded in the process—that has been the hardest part. But slowly, most everyone on the team, which had once been in such trouble, has followed our lead, rising to the next level time and time again. It has now become one of the healthiest teams in our church. Years later, Kenneth has moved on to another ministry role, but the reports of his accomplishments continue to be encouraging. He is working hard on trust, integrity, clarity, and communication—and God is taking him to the top as well.

Conversation #3

TALK IT OVER

After you've read the Chapter on THERE'S NO TEAM WITHOUT TRUST, take a few minutes with your group to talk through some of the questions below. Give everyone a chance to share, and encourage everyone to be honest, authentic, and supportive of others. Always remember to affirm vulnerability and thank those who are willing to share and ask for prayer.

1. Think about some of your experiences in life. Perhaps you are one who has struggled with trust. Can you share an example of what has helped you through the struggle?

2. We all come to the table with differing levels of trust based on things like our experiences, basic temperament, and growth in forgiveness. How can we help each other as team members who may struggle with trust?

3. The experience I shared of working for George (pages 59-60) was that of a supervisor who didn't trust his team. Perhaps you have had a similar experience of a leader who "over-managed" people. Without naming names, share how this made you feel. Were you able to give your best under these conditions?

4. What does credibility look like in everyday life? What are some practical ways we can build credibility with people?

5. When a team lacks candid communication it is a sign that trust is lacking. What things are lost when there is no freedom to be candid within a team? What benefits does candid communication bring? What steps can each of us take to help make our candid communications easier to receive?

6. If you are like me, you see a little bit of yourself in Kenneth's story. What specific area did the Holy Spirit convict you about?

Thank each member of the team who is open and honest enough to share where they are being challenged. Pray for one another asking for the Holy Spirit's help in these areas.

Conversation #3

TEAM UP AND MAKE IT BETTER

Before you end your group conversation...

Clarity enables all members of a team to have a unified focus and work toward a common goal. Spend some time with your team discussing the clarity building questions from this chapter:

- Who are we?

- What do we do?

- How do we do it?

- What does a "win" look like for us?

Sometime before your next conversation...

- Review this chapter and note anything that you've decided to change in your life. Talk to God about it, and make a decision to get started by faith.

- Read the next chapter so you'll be ready to have a great conversation when your group gets together next.

LEADERSHIP TAKE-AWAY #3:

"Healthy Leaders Set the Stage
for Trust on the Team"

This section for leaders is a little longer than the others, but for good reason. First, the ropes of trust secure everything else in a leader's world. Without trust, we ourselves can't climb to the top, much less take anyone with us. Second, I have a huge love and respect for you, my friends in leadership. This is a really hard climb, and it can be overwhelming. I get it, because just like you I am striving to climb.

So before you begin the next stage of your ascent, let me once again sit down next to you, put my arm around you and share my heart. You are key to your team's trust level—there's no other way to say it. It may not be up to you alone, but it is up to you to lead the way. Your role is to set the stage for team trust.

How can a leader begin to do this? Make sure you catch the heart of this chapter, and reread it if it will help. Ask the Lord to speak to you. Then, make sure you have what you need to begin climbing.

Here is a basic checklist to help you set the stage for trust on your team:

1. Make sure you are trusting the right things.

Trust is the foundation of our spiritual lives as well as our leadership. Are you trusting God or your own ability? Are you relying on people, or have you learned to rely on God? The prophet Jeremiah calls us to make sure our trust is correctly placed, saying:

> "Thus says the Lord: 'Cursed is the man who trusts in man and makes flesh his strength, whose heart turns away from the Lord. He is like a shrub in the desert, and shall not see any good come.

74

He shall dwell in the parched places of the wilderness, in an uninhabited salt land. "'Blessed is the man who trusts in the Lord, whose trust is the Lord. He is like a tree planted by water, that sends out its roots by the stream, and does not fear when heat comes, for its leaves remain green, and is not anxious in the year of drought, for it does not cease to bear fruit.'"
JEREMIAH 17:5-8 ESV

To test this, ask yourself, *Am I leading from a place of fear or trust? Am I prone to micromanage like George? Why?* Perhaps you trusted people in the past and they let you down.

Trusting others when they fail you can be harder than climbing the world's highest mountain. I know a pastor who led a remarkable church. He suffered for nine months with the effects of a physical and emotional breakdown due to stress and overwork. Just as he was beginning to recover, he discovered that his wife had been unfaithful to him during his illness. The pain was intense, but he rounded up enough trust and courage to repair his health and his marriage. After some time, he felt strong enough to take another risk. He planted a new church and began in ministry again, putting everything he had into it. Sadly, within a couple of years the church had to be closed. I have prayed often for this man because he is going through more than I can imagine. Will he ever be able to trust again? Thankfully, there is hope and healing in the Lord!

> "May the God of hope fill you with all joy and peace as you *trust* in him, so that you may overflow with hope by the power of the Holy Spirit." ROMANS 15:13 NIV

> "When I am afraid, I put my *trust* in you." PSALM 56:4 NIV

Allow God to restore any injured trust, and receive His grace afresh. It is sufficient for you today!

2. Set an example that is easy for others to trust.

As we've seen in this chapter, credibility is key to any leader's influence. You have credibility as a leader when people believe you are safe, reliable, and always thinking of their needs and perspectives. Being consistent is crucial to earning people's trust. Leadership experts James Kouzes and Barry Posner found in their research that most people's understanding of credible behavior is expressed in the following phrase: *Do what you say you will do (DWYSYWD).* [20]

Jesus is the only leader with perfect credibility. We can only become more trustworthy as we follow Him and operate in His grace. Billy Graham is a shining example of this. He had the kind of character that was easy for people to trust. He simply followed the Lord as best he could. That will work for any leader.

What are your core convictions when it comes to lifestyle? Are you raising the bar to the right level? Are you living out your core convictions? Are you building trust or destroying it with your example?

One of a leader's top jobs in this regard is in getting control of his or her words. I've heard it said that,

A leader's words weigh a thousand pounds.

Each of us will be evaluated by God and others on the basis of our words (Matthew 12:37). So the credibility challenge remains for us to set limits on what we say and how we say it.

"When there are many words, transgression is unavoidable, but he who restrains his lips is wise." PROVERBS 10:19 NASB

"But now you must also rid yourselves of all such things as these: anger, rage, malice, slander, and filthy language from your lips. Do not lie to each other...Clothe yourselves with compassion, kindness, humility, gentleness and patience." COLOSSIANS 3:8-12 NIV

Speak in a way that affirms and encourages. Remember Don

Bennet, the amputee who conquered Mt. Ranier? At one point he described how, during a difficult trek across an ice field, his daughter stayed at his side and with each hop told him, "You can do it, Dad. You're the best dad in the world. You can do it, Dad." He told his interviewers that there was no way he would quit hopping to the top with his daughter yelling words of love and encouragement in his ear. [21] When you cheer for your team, it spurs them to keep trusting and keep climbing to the top.

Reflect on your leadership journey. How have your own mistakes and shortcomings damaged your credibility? How have your strengths, good decisions, and positive actions helped create credibility? With those lessons learned, renew your commitment to set an example everyone can trust.

3. Build a better culture of trust on your team.

Trust thrives when there is clarity. In our church, we have been strong on spiritual gifts, worship, prayer, and teaching. We have discovered, however, that none of these are a substitute for clarity of mission, expectations, and roles. We have renewed our efforts to step up our culture of trust by providing our people with clarity. We're not all the way there, but it is beginning to pay off.

Here are three ideas for increasing clarity on your team and building a culture of trust.

- *Communicate clear expectations.* Part of our challenge in the past had been in assuming that our teams knew what we expected from them. We have been good at recruiting and empowering people, but weak in providing clarity on their roles. Does this sound familiar?

Everyone on the team needs to know their roles and tasks, especially in larger teams and organizations. They need to know who they report to. They need a clear and current position description and an overview of how they fit into the entire organization. The larger the team, the more urgent this becomes.

What organizational structures and systems exist, and how does each team fit into them? What are the values of the organization, and how is this reflected in the structures? Achieving this kind of clarity can be an overwhelming task, but in larger organizations, it cannot be neglected. We found the services of an outside consultant to be helpful in this regard. [22]

- *Conduct regular team reviews.* Great teams are willing to sit down after the game and watch the tape. Honestly evaluating things together may seem scary, but it is very clarifying. Recently I met with our creative team to vision cast for our big Easter Sunday services (which we call Resurrection Sunday). There were some uncomfortable issues brewing within our team related to certain "traditions" that we had relied on in the past but no longer felt like a fit. As we bravely looked at what changes we might need to make, we decided to honestly and openly review three things:

    What have we been doing that is really working?
    What have we been doing that no longer seemed to work well?
    What have we been doing that was "just okay"?

We decided that no matter how long our "sacred cows" had been with us, or how sensitive some might be to changes, we needed to be willing to either change or set aside the things that weren't working. This would free us to amplify the things that *were* working. This agreement of purpose produced freedom and creativity. Our team went to a new level, and we ended up with a much better plan for the most important services of the year.

- *Clarify the pathway of conflict resolution.* Most leaders hate conflict—I know I do. I get triggered just thinking about dissension in the ranks! Perhaps this is because dissension can be so dangerous and destructive to the team. Leaders are builders— they want things to come together, not come unglued. But the truth is that no matter how hard we try, conflicts are inevitable, even on a healthy team. In fact, they are essential to the team's health. If conflict is handled correctly, everyone achieves clarity without breaking the relationships in the process.

It is the job of every team leader to make sure everyone knows how the team resolves conflict. People need to know they can go somewhere safe with their issue. They need to feel that there is a way to bring up a problem without being labeled a problem. As their leader, make sure they can do that. Teach them how and with whom to air their issues in a healthy way. Start by regularly referring to the Matthew 18 model (I will cover this in more detail in the next chapter). Confront divisiveness and runaway conversations when appropriate, but be sure to welcome and celebrate team honesty and reconciliation.

4. Actively weed and water team relationships.

Jesus told this story: "A man planted a fig tree in his garden and came again and again to see if there was any fruit on it, but he was always disappointed. Finally, he said to his gardener, 'I've waited three years, and there hasn't been a single fig! Cut it down. It's just taking up space in the garden.' The gardener answered, 'Sir, give it one more chance. Leave it another year, and I'll give it special attention and plenty of fertilizer. If we get figs next year, fine. If not, then you can cut it down.'"
LUKE 13:6-9 NLT

I like to think of team relationships and trust as a garden I need to keep weeded and watered. As a leader, it is my job to keep my team relationships clear of the weeds that constantly try to overtake them. If I neglect this garden, I will not only be disappointed, I'll be held responsible.

"I walked by the field of a lazy person...It was covered with weeds, and its walls were broken down. Then, as I looked and thought about it, I learned this lesson: A little extra sleep, a little more slumber...then poverty will pounce on you like a bandit; scarcity will attack you like an armed robber."
PROVERBS 24:30-34 NLT

I have noticed a number of weeds that crop up in every team's garden. Which ones have you seen?

- *Miscommunication* is a primary tool of the enemy. He loves to sow the seed of misunderstanding and suspicion. Fight back with clarity in communication and prayer.

- *Trespasses* occur when we "go too far" with others, violating healthy limits and boundaries. Many times, offenses are the result of relational trespasses. Teach and guard healthy boundaries.

- *Unresolved offenses* can lead to division and bitterness on the team. What greater attack can the enemy launch than to sow seeds of offense? Follow the Lord's plan for resolving offenses.

When the trust garden is overgrown with ugly attitudes, suspicions, and fears, it needs attention. Don't get too busy and miss what's happening in your garden. Many a leader has lost relationships on their team and in their family as a result of looking the other way.

Your best role as a leader is to set the stage for team trust, and keep the garden well weeded and watered. Stay focused on the climb ahead, and I'll see you at the top.

THE SYMPHONY OF TEAM AGREEMENT

"Can two walk together, unless they are agreed?"
—THE PROPHET AMOS

When you hear the names Mozart, Beethoven, Dvorak and Tchaikovsky, what comes to mind? Even though they passed away hundreds of years ago, these composers are still celebrated as some of the most brilliant in history. Their vibrant symphonies have inspired the world for centuries. Who could ignore the majesty of Mozart's 41st, resist the beauty of Beethoven's 3rd, or forget the power Tchaikovsky's 5th? Their compositions transport us, inspire us—even move us to tears.

What is it about a symphony that is so majestic? Why does the sound of an orchestra move us so deeply? I was discussing this with my nephew, Dr. Zackary Bruno, Professor of Music and Director of Bands and Orchestras at Skyline College in San Bruno, California. Zack is an accomplished symphony conductor who has honed his craft alongside some of the greatest conductors in America.

"I believe the answer is resonance, Uncle David," he explained. "There are deep vibrations in pure sound. When conditions are right, the sound of an orchestra moves through the atmosphere of a concert hall, funneling through your senses and flooding your nervous system with sublime pleasure. That is resonance, and there's nothing else like it."

As he continued to describe the impact of sound and music, using

81

terms like "sympathetic vibrations" and the "exquisite perfection of the composer's vision," I struggled to take it all in. One thing that really stood out in Zack's remarks, however, was this: the powerful impact of a musical performance when it achieves *unison.*

Unison is that magical moment in music when performance becomes perfection. The word itself comes from an old French word meaning "one sound"—and that's exactly how Zack described it: "Unison is that one sound which flows from many instruments simultaneously to create performance perfection. In unison, there is no discord or dissonance." He continued,

> *"Everything comes together in perfect musical agreement."*

Upon hearing the word "agreement," I immediately got goose bumps. Agreement is one of the most important qualities any healthy team can have, and it's the main concept of this chapter. "What do you mean by musical agreement?" I eagerly asked. He explained, "You could say it's when everything gels musically and just comes together. In unison, pitch and timing are on, tone is perfect, musicians are pulling together, and everything is blending into one, seamless sound. This is when the music really resonates."

Then, after a moment's pause, Zack continued slowly, almost reverently: "Uncle David, there is a moment at the end of a perfect performance, as the final note of a piece slowly fades into silence, that for just a few seconds, that note actually rings in the atmosphere. We call this 'ringing true,' and for me as a symphony conductor, it is the height of musical perfection."

Agreement, unison, resonance—Zack was giving me a new vocabulary for teamwork. In this chapter, let's use that vocabulary to talk about team agreement and what it can mean for your life.

DISCOVERING AGREEMENT

I heard about a couple—let's call them Harry and Adele—who were celebrating their 60th wedding anniversary. At their party, everyone was dancing, laughing, and enjoying great food. Toward the end of the evening, it was time for them to share a few words with their honored guests. Adele was known to have the stronger personality, so no one was surprised when she took the microphone first. As she thanked her guests for coming, someone in the back shouted, "How did you two stay married for so many years?" She responded with characteristic spunk, giving all the married couples her clear-eyed counsel for their relationships.

It was now Harry's turn to speak, and, being a quiet man, he described their partnership from his perspective: "When Adele and I were first married, we made a simple agreement that we have kept for all these years. The agreement is that after we discuss things, I would always make the major decisions, and she would always make the minor decisions." Many were surprised that someone as strong as Adele would allow Harry to make the big decisions alone. His pause allowed the irony to hang in the air for a moment before he continued: "...And in 60 years of those discussions, it's amazing—we've never had to make even one major decision!" The crowd erupted in laughter, including Adele, and everyone understood how agreement became the "secret" to their success!

What is an agreement, naturally speaking? Today, as throughout history, an agreement is simply a mutually beneficial arrangement between parties. For example, our country makes trade agreements with other nations. These agreements govern the flow of commerce between nations for the benefit of the parties included in the agreement. Married couples, business partners, neighbors, and team members can all benefit from agreements. Without an agreement, we don't get the intended benefits.

When the ancient Hebrew prophet Amos posed the famous question which challenged Israel's unfaithfulness to God, he was speaking of something beyond the natural level of agreement—He was calling for *spiritual agreement*: "Can two walk together, unless they are *agreed?*" (Amos 3:3). This kind of agreement is the essence of what we could call spiritual unison. Israel needed to return to true unity with their God.

Amos chose his words wisely. The Hebrew word translated "agreement" is *ya'ad,* which means, "to arrive together." The imagery is of walking together on a journey. Amos wants people to walk together with God and arrive at the place of blessing and fruitfulness He has destined for them. This kind of agreement begins with our mind and heart, and ultimately takes us somewhere. Agreement is an intentional journey—with each step, there is intention, purpose and the anticipation of blessing.

THE AWESOME POTENTIAL OF AGREEMENT

The conversation with my nephew ignited my thoughts on healthy teamwork. I realized that good teams are like good orchestras—a collection of individual contributors with unique abilities coming together in agreement to accomplish something that they could never do alone.

> *Agreement is an indispensable quality on any healthy team.*

If your team could function in the kind of agreement like that of a great orchestra, what could it mean for you and your mission? As I reflected on Zack's words, I realized that the potential of agreement on a team would mirror that of a symphony in three ways.

• *Agreement releases power*

Zack's description of the final note in a symphony "ringing true" was weighty, and it reinforced my belief that,

> *Anything done in unison has the*
> *power to move heaven and earth.*

Our conversation took me back to the promise of Jesus concerning agreement in prayer:

84

"Again I say to you that if two of you *agree* on earth concerning anything that they ask, it will be done for them by My Father in heaven." MATTHEW 18:19

The Greek word in this verse which has been correctly translated "agree" is *sumphoneo,* which is related to our word "symphony." It means to "make the same sound together." Jesus implies that as we come together in agreement, our prayers become a symphony before God's throne. God is deeply moved by the ring of agreement in prayer. In response, He releases the incredible power of the Holy Spirit to move heaven and earth on our behalf!

Could this be the same powerful sound that resonated in the early church?

"When the Day of Pentecost had fully come, they were all *with one accord in one place.* And suddenly there came *a sound from heaven,* as of a rushing mighty wind... And they were all filled with the Holy Spirit." ACTS 2:1-4 NKJV

The inspiring phrase, "in one accord" occurs a total of five times in the Book of Acts. Each time, we get a clearer picture of what God's power looks like when we come together in agreement: *The power of the Holy Spirit fell,* (Acts 2:1-4), *the church grew and multiplied* (2:41-47), *people became bold* (4:23-31), *"great grace came upon them"* (4:32), and they experienced *signs and wonders* (5:12). The clear message is about the awesome potential of agreement.

When I teach on the potential of agreement, I always remind people of what I heard my good friend Pastor Ed Delph teach years ago:

The place of agreement is the place of power.

"There is nothing else on earth like agreement," Ed will often say. "If a church or a team has zero agreement, they have zero power. Increase your agreement to fifty percent, and you'll have fifty percent power. Bring your agreement to one hundred percent—to the kind of agreement described by Jesus and in the Book of Acts—

and you'll have one hundred percent power!"

- *Agreement creates pleasure*

Zack's passion soared as he explained the joy of a perfect performance. I recalled my own moments of joy in life: my first date with Kathy, our wedding day, the birth of our children, and so many more. Agreement sets the stage for life's most joyful moments, but it also makes life's mundane moments easier.

Years ago, as an undergraduate student, I discovered the benefits of listening to recorded symphonies as I studied. I found them energizing and enlightening. The delight of the music made the drudgery of the mundane more bearable. Not that I was a great connoisseur of the arts—despite years of vocal classes in school and private piano lessons, I never accomplished much more than a few basics as a musician. But like with many people, great music has always brought me joy. Whether it is sacred or secular, classic old-school Rock, Gospel, R & B, or Hawaiian, when you experience something that rings true, it brings pleasure.

As Zack continued to explain musical agreement, I realized what a gift agreement is, and how much pleasure it brings to relationships. For example, while my marriage to Kathy is far from perfect, the reason it's been so pleasurable is because we have stayed in agreement. That's not to say we have always seen eye to eye on everything—we often have very different desires and perspectives. But we never make a move until we are in agreement. The symphony of agreement in our lives has made our relationship more enjoyable than I could ever have imagined.

- *Agreement fulfills purpose*

The most important reward for agreement is the fulfillment of a team's purpose. Whether it's a ministry team or an orchestra,

Without agreement, there can be no symphony.

Think about the purpose of a symphony orchestra: it brings diverse instruments together to produce a musical masterpiece. Each member of the orchestra plays a part, and together, they create something incredible.

We don't have to think or believe in exactly the same ways in order to experience agreement. In a symphony, the majestic sound is the result of distinct instruments agreeing. As Zack explained, "In an orchestra, you have different instruments and different mechanisms by which they make sound. Percussionists add to the symphony by striking something. The brass instruments come alive through the buzzing of the lips. The strings make their sound by scraping horsehair bows across metal wires, while the woodwinds gently force air across a wooden reed." In life, as in a symphony, our differences are not the issue—our ability to walk in agreement is.

Whatever the team, when we are humble and available, the Holy Spirit harmonizes us, blending our spiritual gifts together to fulfill God's purpose.

WHEN MANY BECOME ONE

I searched my memory. "Zack, I remember reading about some findings that were presented years ago at a meeting of the American Psychological Association. [23] It was about how members of major symphony orchestras perceived each other. It was reported that percussionists were most often seen as insensitive, string players were viewed as arrogant, brass players were regarded as overbearing and woodwind players were seen as meticulous and sometimes egotistical." Zack laughed out loud because he knew those kinds of perceptions were common.

"Uncle David, it is important to be different; that's what symphony is all about. But thinking about others negatively because they are different from us is never helpful. Sooner or later you have to find common ground if you're going to make great music together."

Zack was right. A symphony is a perfect picture of many becoming one. My mind went to the diversity I've enjoyed living and ministering in the San Francisco Bay Area. My ministry here has been strengthened by the power of agreement between different kinds of leaders. None of us has it all, but as we come together across denominational lines, traditions, and cultures, we see the benefits of being in one accord begin to take shape.

In fact, though we are different, we are becoming something like a family. This makes sense because we were all bought by the blood of Jesus and born into His household. "There is one body, and one Spirit...But unto every one of us is given grace according to the measure of the gift of Christ." EPHESIANS 4:4-7 NKJV

I feel blessed to have experienced the power of agreement with different spiritual leaders in our area, and I can sense the Lord's pleasure in it. He taught us to be peacemakers and bridge-builders in a broken world (Matthew 5:9), and then He prayed for us to be one:

> "My prayer is...that all of them may be one, Father, just as you are in me and I am in you. May they also be in us so that the world may believe that you have sent me. I have given them the glory that you gave me, *that they may be one as we are one*— I in them and you in me—so that they may be brought to *complete unity*. Then the world will know that you sent me and have loved them even as you have loved me." JOHN 17:20-23 NIV

Jesus understood better than anyone that agreement releases the power, pleasure, and purpose of God in our lives, filling us with a glorious sound that resonates in heaven and earth.

WHAT BLOCKS TEAM AGREEMENT?

The parallels between teams and symphonies were growing clearer, but I still needed to get some more answers. "Zack, what barriers to a perfect performance have you faced? With so many variables to deal with—different musicians, venues, acoustical factors, and time constraints—what are the biggest obstacles to agreement?" It didn't take him long to answer. "It's the members of the orchestra, Uncle David. Pure and simple, we are our own biggest enemies." My wise nephew confirmed what I'd already seen:

*The barriers to agreement are hidden deep in
the hearts of the members of the team.*

Zack continued, "In my experience, orchestra members can carry issues deep inside that affect their ability to gel with others in the orchestra. These attitudes affect our performance so much, my role has become part leader, part musician, and part psychologist." We both laughed. As a pastor, I could relate.

He then lamented about how many times he had seen anger and bitterness destroy musical potential. "I know musicians who have lost their love of music because of disappointments with their careers. Their attitude is, 'This orchestra isn't good enough for me—I was supposed to be better than this!'"

"I know what you mean, Zack—I've seen it in ministry as well." I thought about so many I have known who lost the joy of serving God because they allowed an attitude to take root in their heart.

"The bottom line on agreement is this," Zack concluded. "It would be impossible for an orchestra to come together and make great music unless each member of the team can master their attitudes and pull together as one."

I recalled an example from many years ago of how the heart affects teamwork. "This was long before you were born, Zack, but in 1967, the Beatles were the greatest musical group the world had ever seen, One of their most famous songs was 'All you need is love'." Zack knew the song but not the story.

I continued, "That song was at the top of the charts, and my generation really believed those lyrics. Then in 1969, two years after that song's release, the Beatles announced they were breaking up! We all thought, 'What? Wait! What happened to *All you need is love?*'" One of the greatest musical teams in history came apart because of the issues in their hearts. We laughed at the irony, but quickly realized,

> *If agreement isn't first in our hearts,*
> *it will never work on the team.*

Which leads us to the question, What specific heart attitudes might block the flow of unity and agreement? I have discovered that a few common attitudes can break up the band quicker than anything.

- *Self-importance blocks agreement.*

It is reported that Leonard Bernstein, the celebrated orchestra conductor, was once asked, "What is the hardest instrument to play?" Without a moment's hesitation he replied, "Second fiddle. I can always get plenty of first violinists. But to find one who plays second violin with as much enthusiasm...now that's a problem! And yet if no one plays second, we have no harmony." [24]

When it comes to team unity, pride may well be the most damaging of all sins. Whether we are a conductor or an instrumentalist—a team leader or a team member—pride secretly seduces us into the "love of preeminence," as it did with Diotrephes (3 John 9-10). Pride whispers permission to entertain competitive or comparing attitudes. It assures us that our opinions are always correct—that we never need to give another way of doing things a second thought.

Zack reminded me that nothing reveals pride more than a *prima donna* attitude. "A prima donna is someone who acts like they are the star of the show," he said. "They feel entitled to special attention or treatment because of their ability. This always throws a wet blanket on the team."

Thankfully, true humility has the power to take us beyond our prideful attitudes and the discord that always follows. Great team members focus on the importance of the team, not on themselves.

- *Divisiveness blocks agreement.*

Divisiveness is the opposite of being "in one accord." Paul urged the divided believers in Corinth, "Come together in agreement. Do not allow anything or anyone to create division among you. Instead, be restored, completely fastened together with one mind and shared judgment." 1 CORINTHIANS 1:10-12, TVT

Fighting, schism, and division are the sour notes that ruin a symphony of agreement. I was recently reading about the Hatfields and the McCoys, whose feud became legendary in American history. Lasting from 1863 to 1891, the fight between two families began over a stolen hog. A civil trial only made the rift deeper, and so the fighting began.

It all came to a bloody climax in the New Year's Massacre of 1888, when a group of Hatfields surrounded the home of one sleeping Randolph McCoy in the middle of the night, and released a hail of bullets. Two of his children died, though he and his wife barely escaped. The schism had become so violent that the United States government had to get involved. Eventually, eight Hatfields got life in prison, and one was executed. After that, the feud died out, but the question still remains, why did they allow their differences to bring about so much damage?

A healthy team can be patient with many things, but it cannot afford to go easy on divisive people. To sound like a symphony, we must deal with any discord before it brings damage to the team.

- *A lack of love blocks agreement.*

In any team, skills and commitment are important. As we've seen, communication, trust, and honesty are key. And no team does well without everyone "buying in" to the vision and flowing with the team leader. But there is one note that really pulls the symphony of a team together:

"Though I speak with the tongues of men and of angels, but

have not love, I have become a sounding brass or a clanging cymbal . . .." 1 CORINTHIANS 13:1 NKJV

Without love, the best orchestra will be out of tune. Rick Renner describes Paul's statement:

> "...Paul encountered a group of people who were extremely 'super-spiritual' in the city of Corinth. However, he was unimpressed with these people and their level of spirituality because they had an obvious lack of love...The illustration Paul chose to use was the endless, nonstop, annoying, aggravating, irritating, frenzied beating and clanging of brass that was performed in pagan worship and that echoed ceaselessly throughout the city of Corinth. The citizens of Corinth could never escape the endless banging of this metal..." [25]

Hardly a symphony, right? Yet that's what any team sounds like when they lack love. Love is the reason we are able to agree and create a symphony together. You can have a room full of skillful, perfectly prepared musicians, but that doesn't make them an orchestra. Nothing rings true until we are filled with the love of God for one another.

HOPE FOR HEALTHY TEAMS

There is hope for our hearts to change so that we can experience the symphony of team agreement.

The story is told of some young prophets who were studying with Elisha. [26] They became hungry and someone put on a pot of stew. A stew is a combination of different ingredients simmering together over time to create a pleasing flavor. But when one of them mistakenly added some wild gourds to the stew, it became poisonous. The hungry students called for Elisha's help, saying, "There is death in the pot!" He instructed them to throw some flour into the stew, and the stew was miraculously healed.

The main lesson in this story is that God can heal what has become poisoned. Through Jesus Christ, who was symbolically ground into fine flour for our sins, the poison in our world can be removed and we can be nourished, Praise the Lord!

But there is another application: A team is like a pot of stew. They are made up of different kinds of people, with different abilities. As they blend together, the aroma is pleasing. When we allow a wild attitude to secretly poison the team, the stew becomes unhealthy, but if we add the heart of Jesus to a team, the poison is removed and the team becomes safe.

No matter what kind team we're looking at—a marriage, a family or a ministry—the love of Jesus Christ can heal it. Don't throw a tainted team away. Infuse it with love, and let God redeem it. When we have love, we can honor each other and find the strength to be patient. When we love, we can forgive each other. And with Jesus as our Conductor, there is always hope for harmony.

FOUR CHORDS OF TEAM AGREEMENT

When a conductor steps in front of an orchestra, he or she has a lot to accomplish. Whether it is in the first rehearsal or the final performance, the conductor will begin by raising the baton and then launching the musicians into their various roles at the proper time. The conductor will use every means available to bring the group into unison; face, arms, eyes—the entire body is moving. The directions must be clear to each member of the orchestra throughout the performance.

In this intricate process, nothing is more important than insuring that each instrumentalist follows the score. The score is the sheet music that contains all the language and notations that give direction to the piece being performed. A score uses musical notes and chords, tempos, rhythms, *crescendos* and *decrescendos*, and much more to spell out the details that each instrumentalist needs to succeed. Following the score and the leadership of the conductor, everyone plays their part with confidence and adds their contribution to the whole.

In much the same way, healthy teams need clear guidelines to shape the team's performance—rules and standards that mold the team's behavior, relationships, and attitudes. Depending on the nature of the team, these can be written as formal agreements that everyone reads and signs when they join the team, or they can be shared less formally. [27] A team agreement, whether it is written or not, is about making sure we keep the promises we make in joining and serving on our team. Everyone on the team should understand what the team is all about and what matters most at any given moment. A wise leader brings his or her team back to the team agreement, much as a symphony conductor brings his orchestra to their score.

The following four chords of team agreement will serve any team well, but are not a complete song. They would be basic starting points for any team, but no substitute for the unique song your team needs to write together.

TEAM AGREEMENT #1 - *"We agree to honor everyone consistently."*

This first chord is a major chord. In chapter two, we talked about the importance of honor in any relationship. No one appreciates being disrespected on a team or anywhere else in life. If we disrespect those whom God has called us to work with, the team will become unhealthy. When we truly honor each other, we are adding to the symphony of team agreement.

Peter's instructions to the early church were clear: "Honor everyone. Love the brotherhood. Fear God. Honor the emperor" (1 Peter 2:17, ESV). What does it mean to honor someone, whether they are a brother, team-member, or political leader? At its core, it means to gratefully and openly acknowledge two things:

- *Who they have been created by God to be.* God has given everyone unique traits. Each of us has the gifts, personality, style, gender, and ethnicity that God knew would be best. Like a fine instrument, each of us are hand-crafted by God according to His purposes. Even our limitations are a part of God's design. When we celebrate those unique traits, and allow others to be who they are, more than who we wish they were, we are honoring one another as well as the Lord.

- *The position that God has given them in your life.* "We also need to acknowledge where God has placed us in each other's lives." We are all equally valuable, but not all of us have the same function. 1 Corinthians 12:18 says, "God has set the members, each one of them, in the body just as He pleased." Some are conductors, others percussionists or section-leaders. When we honor the places that our leaders, spouses, parents, friends, and team members have been given in our lives, we are honoring the Lord as well as them, and putting ourselves in a position to experience agreement and unison.

Honoring is a difficult chord to play. When it comes to dishonoring, we don't even have to try—it's easy! But honoring others takes intentionality and practice. In His famous "Golden Rule," Jesus points us to the best way to honor others consistently: "Therefore, whatever you want men to do to you, do also to them, for this is the Law and the Prophets" (Matthew 7:12). This challenging commitment requires us to be humble and selfless, as Paul noted:

> "Be of the same mind, by having the same love, being united in spirit, and having one purpose. Instead of being motivated by selfish ambition or vanity, each of you should, in humility, be moved to treat one another as more important than yourself." PHILIPPIANS 2:2-5 NET

This kind of honor is so powerful that it can turn our relationships around. A tearful wife told me recently how she had complained for years about her husband's unique personality. He wasn't anything like what she thought he should be. Finally, she decided to humble herself, let go of her gripes and honor him as publicly as

95

she had complained about him. It was a complete game-changer for their marriage. Today they are walking in agreement. Remember, whatever you honor moves toward you and whatever you dishonor moves further away.

TEAM AGREEMENT #2 - *"We agree to resolve team conflicts constructively."*

The second chord is a progression toward a beautiful resolution. In chapter 2, we also touched on the inevitability of conflict on a team. We are human, so there are going to be challenges in any marriage, friendship, or team. We have an enemy, and he is constantly working to divide us. I know a pastor who also had a counseling practice. He literally wrote a book on being in one accord, yet he left his church because of an unresolved offense with his lead pastor. What a tragic failure for his team! It could have been avoided if both had honored the team enough to resolve their issues constructively.

In Matthew 18:15, Jesus spelled out the clearest call in all of Scripture for us to walk in reconciliation: "If your brother sins against you, go and tell him his fault between you and him alone. If he hears you, you have gained your brother." When it's time to clear up a conflict, practicing four principles will fully protect the process.

- *Be Honest.* Jesus said, "Go and tell him his fault" because we need to be honest with ourselves and those who have offended us. It is both dishonest and dangerous to pretend that we are not offended. If a valid issue has come up, we should approach our offender (Proverbs 27:5), and be ready to own our part of the problem as well. As you share your concern, attack the problem not the person, and focus on common ground.

- *Be Discrete.* Jesus said the problem is to be solved "between you and him alone." We need to keep others out of it. Gossip and tale-bearing may masquerade as something more refined like "sharing" or a "prayer request," but they're both still sinful (2

Corinthians 12:20). Involving others undermines agreement. A good rule of thumb is to talk TO each other, not ABOUT each other. This will protect everyone and preserve agreement on the team.

- *Be a Listener.* Jesus' words "If he hears you" raise the issue of our responsibility to listen with a humble heart. "Be slow to speak, quick to listen..." (James 1:19). After listening, apologies can be made. If you respond rather than react to what you are hearing, you'll avoid an escalation of emotion that threatens harmony. Be quick to apologize—it'll cost you nothing but your pride. Then mutual forgiveness can be extended, and the relationship will be saved. If your words are ignored, take it to God in prayer and try another approach. But never forget: we are responsible to be good listeners in our relationships (Matthew 5:23-25).

- *Be a Reconciler.* Jesus defined success with the words, "...You have gained your brother." The goal of honest confrontation is to restore the relationship, not damage it. Think and pray before you speak. Don't let your tongue start a fire your team can't put out. Aim for win-win outcomes, where nobody walks away in shame or rejection.

On a team, there will always be opportunities for offenses, misunderstandings, miscommunications, and hurt feelings no matter how hard we try. But when we agree to resolve our conflicts in the right way, we preserve team health and protect everyone on the team.

TEAM AGREEMENT #3 - *"We agree to champion the vision enthusiastically."*

Our third chord of agreement helps by creating a clear sound. Every team needs a purpose and vision that every team member can believe in and be inspired by. Our shared aspirations are what make or break our teams. When there is no clear vision to agree on, it's hard to function. But when there is a clear purpose in front of each member of the team, a sense of agreement kicks in and helps everyone achieve it together.

A clear vision statement would answer the following basic questions:

- *Who are we?* Are we a leadership team, a worship team, a healing team? It may seem simple, but without understanding who you are and how you fit into the organization as a whole, you can't define your function. For example, our church defines who we are by stating, "We are a church for all people." This signals identity—who we are and who we are not. We are a community of faith where everyone is welcome to join us in discovering and following Jesus together. Who is *your* team?

- *What do we do?* Every team needs a clear mission, including tasks and responsibilities. Don't take for granted that your team knows what these are. Everyone should have a clear idea of what needs to happen and when it needs to happen. Each person on the team needs a simple job description as well. In our church, our broad mission is *Inspiring Transformed Lives*—which means we live to see people's lives lifted and changed by the power of God. What does *your* team do?

- *Why do we do it?* Every team needs an answer to the question, why? Why do we rehearse, serve, give, honor, reconcile, and work faithfully? Many times, people lose their motivation because they forget their *why*. Great leaders reinforce the *why*. In our church, we build everything on the *why* of honoring God—we do what we do to honor God because He is worthy. We also talk about loving people as one of our *whys*. We serve because we want people to be saved, healed, freed, and fulfilled. Why does *your* team do what it does?

- *How do we do it?* Healthy teams need to agree on their approach. How do we greet, run sound, lead worship or lead youth? When there is confusion on this, the team cannot be in agreement. For example, one youth ministry might use a combination of small relational groups and larger, high-energy atmospheres to reach teenagers. Another youth ministry might choose sports programs and weekly line-by-line Bible studies. How does *your* team function?

Once a team has a clear and inspiring vision for everyone to agree on, it is important to champion that vision regularly. The goal is that each and every member of the team is buying in to the vision and owning it. Healthy teams are made up of people who champion the vision and encourage each other. Each member of the team sees his or herself as an investor, not merely a volunteer. They champion the vision together.

Here are some practical ways you can champion the vision you are a part of: Love the vision, believe in it, pray for it, and represent it well. Never speak disparagingly of your team; its leadership or its progress. If you have a concern, take it to God in prayer. Love your team like it's a part of Christ's family, because it is. No team is perfect, but believe that God is using your team and making it better. Most of all, know and celebrate the *who, what, why,* and *how* of your team! As you do, you'll be adding to the symphony of team agreement and inspiring everyone around you.

TEAM AGREEMENT #4 - *"We agree to keep our commitments faithfully."*

The final chord is about faithfulness. It's a chord that needs to be held and sustained for more than a few measures.

Henry was such a great guy. He was friendly, outgoing, and always smiling. All of us just loved Henry, and he loved the team—or so we thought. The problem with Henry was his commitment to the team. Henry wasn't reliable. His assignments were always falling through the cracks. He never wrote important things down, and rarely remembered to follow through. He was always running late, and sometimes he didn't show up at all.

Henry was so friendly that we put up with his faults for longer than we should have. At times, we would communicate our concerns with his bad habits, and every time, Henry let us know how awful he felt. He agreed to change, but continued to fail the team. We hated the thought of removing him, so for a time, we begged and pleaded. Henry was always so nice about apologizing and promising to do better that we gave him lots of chances.

Unfortunately, Henry never really committed to the team. There was nothing left to do but replace him with someone who would take the team seriously.

It takes more than friendship to function on a team. In *The Wisdom of Teams*, Jon R. Katzenbach and Douglas K. Smith say it best:

"The essence of a team is common commitment." [28]

Faithfulness to our commitments is a part of team agreement. No team can develop trust or perform well apart from a shared commitment to doing the work and accomplishing the tasks, goals, and responsibilities of their position on the team.

The Lord expects us to be faithful, even in small things (Luke 16:10). On a team, everyone should do real work, pull their weight, and do whatever it takes as a team to get the job done. No one should slack, no matter the position or how long they have been a part. No matter how friendly they are, people who lack the commitment to be faithful cannot stay long on a healthy team.

Keeping these four team agreements in mind, your team can begin to take the next steps in your journey toward the symphony of team agreement. You won't get there overnight, but if you walk together in the same direction, you'll arrive at your destination and achieve your dreams. As you travel, you will not be alone. You'll have your team, and most importantly, the Lord will walk with you. Here's a promise to remember as you travel to your place of agreement:

"The Lord directs the steps of the godly. He delights in every detail of their lives. Though they stumble, they will never fall, for the Lord holds them by the hand...Put your hope in the Lord. Travel steadily along his path. He will honor you by giving you the land." PSALMS 27:23-24, 34 NLT

Our insightful discussion was now wrapping up, but I had one final question for my nephew, the conductor. "So Zack, what is team success really about in your mind?" He thought deeply, and answered with assurance: "It's as simple as everyone pulling on the same end of the rope. It's everyone sharing the work and everyone getting the reward. For musicians, that happens when a symphony rings true. But no matter what kind of team it is, if the team is serving God, it is the exact same goal: in the end we all just want to faithfully reflect the composer's vision."

Amen, Zack. May every team make that journey and reach that destination.

Conversation #4

TALK IT OVER

After you've read the Chapter on THE SYMPHONY OF TEAM AGREEMENT, take a few minutes with your group to freely discuss the questions below. Give everyone a chance to share, and encourage everyone to be honest, authentic and supportive of others. As always, remember to affirm vulnerability and thank those who are willing to share and ask for prayer.

1. My conversation with Zack provided me with a new vocabulary for teamwork. Think about the terms agreement, unison, and resonance. Chances are your team is quite different from a symphony orchestra. How can your team achieve the unison of "one sound"? What would it look like for everything to come together in perfect agreement on a team like yours?

2. The prophet Amos speaks of agreement as walking together on a journey (Amos 3:3). If you have ever taken a vacation with your family, you know that disagreements can easily arise while traveling with others. How can team members prevent inevitable disagreements from hindering the group's ability "to arrive together"? What can leaders do to help team members stay focused on the destination?

3. What is the difference between being of the same opinion and being in agreement? Is it possible to have the same opinion and still not be in agreement? Can team members hold differing opinions and perspectives on a matter and still reach agreement? Talk about how this can be achieved on a team.

4. On a team, it is natural for us to have a greater understanding of our particular part and to desire others to appreciate its value. We have to be careful, though, because pride can take advantage of each of us. When we want our piece to stand out, agreement can be lost. What would happen in an orchestra if everyone wanted their part to stand out? What kind of sound would be produced? How can we guard our hearts against the threat of self-importance?

5. One of the blocks to agreement is divisiveness. What is the difference between having a normal disagreement and being divisive? What are some of the roots of divisiveness? What tools has the Lord provided for us to deal with a divisive attitude if we find it in our hearts or on our team?

6. Another block to agreement is a lack of love. Review the attributes of love found in 1 Corinthians 13:4-7. How do these attributes help teams work together effectively? What impact can this kind of love have on how individual members feel about themselves and being on the team? What about the absence of the love attributes? What kind of experience would you expect to have on a team that lacks love?

7. Honor is crucially important to all godly relationships and healthy teams. If you have been blessed with a relationship where honor has been present, talk about this relationship with your group. How did being honored make you feel about yourself? The relationship? Your abilities and potential for success? Talk about the connection between a culture of honor and team productivity.

TEAM UP AND MAKE IT BETTER

Before you end your group conversation...

- Connection to the *why* is important to keep team members engaged and enthusiastic about the team. Take a few minutes to discuss the *whys* of your team. What practical things can team members do to keep the *why* of love in the forefront? How can team leaders consistently reinforce the *why*, so that momentum and motivation are not lost?

- Review the team agreements on pages 94-101. Discuss what these agreements look like on your team specifically. Make a commitment to the Lord and one another. Take the matter to the Lord in prayer, requesting His help in keeping them, and thanking Him for His grace and forgiveness as you collectively and individually strive toward these goals.

Sometime before your next conversation...

- We tend to think that the blocks to agreement are the differences between team members. The reality, however, is "the barriers to agreement are hidden deep in the hearts of the members of the team" (page 89). Consider the three heart attitudes discussed that can block agreement (self-importance, divisiveness, and lack of love). If we are perfectly honest, we have all struggled to some degree with each of these issues. Ask the Lord which area is the biggest challenge to your piece of the team "agreement pie" right now. Repent and ask the Lord for His help, making it a matter of prayer over the next few days.

- When conflicts remain unresolved, they can create relational problems on the team, especially when offense is involved. Review the principles for resolving conflict on pages 96-97 and decide if there are any unresolved offenses you need to privately address. Pray about having a reconciling conversation with anyone you need to.

- Read the next chapter so you'll be ready to have a great conversation when your group gets back together.

LEADERSHIP TAKE-AWAY #4:

Healthy Leaders Wisely Manage Team Agreement.

I've often said that leadership can feel like herding cats. My nephew Zack found that to be true in his role as a symphony conductor. He had to multitask between three roles—musician, leader, and psychologist—because it's a challenge to keep everyone in the orchestra getting along. Can you relate?

As a leader, one of your hardest tasks is to manage agreement on your team, but how do you do that? And what about the difficult people that every leader must inevitably work with—the ones who just don't seem to ever be agreeable?

When it comes to managing agreement on your team, three things will help you as a leader:

1. Make sure your team prays together regularly.

Let God birth a spirit of agreement on your team supernaturally! A prayerless team will have lots of issues. The enemy is working against you. Don't forget to wage the unseen war so you can see the visible blessings God has for your team.

2. Keep communicating the "why" of your ministry.

Overdo vision. I have found that sharing *what we do* and *why we do it* is tremendously unifying. When people forget the why, they get weary, focus on petty differences, and lose the heart of agreement. Don't let that happen. Repaint the fence of vision often—keep it clean and pristine so people will always admire it.

3. Don't overdo your "how" discussions.

Vision unites, but when it comes to strategy— the *how* of accomplishing the vision—disagreement can develop if you are debating methodology too much. There is something wrong with every strategy. Don't get stuck endlessly debating it. Talk strategy with your most trusted team members, and then lead the whole team in the way you see best.

When it comes to dealing with especially difficult team members, the words of Jesus are a gold mine. He not only taught that we should *pray* in agreement (Matthew 18:19), but that we should also *live* in agreement:

> "Therefore if you bring your gift to the altar, and there remember that your brother has something against you, leave your gift there before the altar, and go your way. First *be reconciled* to your brother, and then come and offer your gift. *Agree with your adversary quickly*, while you are on the way with him, lest your adversary deliver you to the judge, the judge hand you over to the officer, and you be thrown into prison." MATTHEW 5:23-25 NKJV EMPHASIS ADDED

What is Jesus trying to teach us about relationships and living in agreement?

- *Life is about conflict and reconciliation.* He knew there would be disagreeable people in our path, so He told us to live as reconcilers. He said before we even worship, our relationships must be right. Jesus is a peacemaker and He has called us to be peacemakers, not provocateurs. Don't be discouraged when there is disagreement. Expect it, and work on reconciliation when needed.

- *We should be the kind of people that can agree with an enemy.* What, you say? It's true! Of course, He's not implying we should part with our core convictions. He's saying that we should be eager to be at peace, always searching for common ground. An agreeable person will "settle it on the courthouse steps" because they know that pressing it all the way to a fight in court will be costly and perhaps end unfavorably. Be careful that you are not so rigid in your principles that you provoke disagreement. Have convictions, but be flexible and put the relationship first. Many of our "convictions" are not worth the fight—just ask one of the Hatfields or McCoys.

Of course, we must never allow ourselves to come into agreement with anything that is directly opposed to God.

"Do not become partners with those who do not believe, for what partnership is there between righteousness and lawlessness, or what fellowship does light have with darkness? And what agreement does Christ have with Belial? ...And what mutual agreement does the temple of God have with idols? Therefore 'come out from their midst, and be separate,' says the Lord, 'and touch no unclean thing, and I will welcome you, and I will be a father to you, and you will be my sons and daughters,' says the All-Powerful Lord." 2 CORINTHIANS 6:14-18 NET

A life of agreement is not a life of compromise.
It is the life of a Christian.

Still, we must be careful not to lose a relationship over a matter that can be compromised on. We can agree to disagree, and that's a form of agreement.

If your best efforts to live in agreement are unsuccessful, here is the counsel of Paul, and the best advice I can give you:

> "If it is possible, as far as it depends on you, live at peace with everyone." ROMANS 12:18 NIV

It may not always be possible to work with everyone, and that's fine. Do your best, and if you can't work with someone, be honest with them. It's okay to say, "We are both trying to walk in agreement here, but it is just not working. Maybe you should pray about being a part of another team." Be careful not to damage the person or reject them personally. Remember, a leader's words weigh a thousand pounds. Affirm them and help them find a better fit somewhere else. In the end, that may be the best way to keep the symphony from brassy discord.

Conversation #5

EVEN HEROES NEED TRAINING

*"I hated every minute of training, but I said, 'Don't quit.
Suffer now and live the rest of your life as a champion.'"*
— MUHAMMAD ALI

Osama Bin Laden had been on the FBI's "Most Wanted" list for
more than a decade. Year after year, the brutal terrorist responsible
for thousands of dead Americans had evaded every effort to capture
and bring him to justice. He had masterminded the horrific 1998
bombings of the U.S. Embassies in Kenya and Tanzania, and the
bloody October 2000 attack of the USS Cole in Yemen's Aden
harbor. But his most savage strike was against the people of the
United States on their own soil: the September 11, 2001, attacks on
the Pentagon in Washington DC and New York's World Trade
Center.

For ten long years, our top intelligence teams scoured the earth in a
futile search for him. Then a break came in August 2010, when the
CIA traced bin Laden to a secure compound in Abbottabad,
Pakistan, 35 miles from the capital of Islamabad. For the next
several months, CIA agents on the ground kept watch on the
compound while drones surveilled it from the sky.

Certain that Bin Laden was there, in March of 2011, President
Barack Obama authorized a plan to reduce the compound to rubble.
US B2 stealth bombers would drop 2,000-pound bombs directly on
his hideout, delivering final justice for those whose lives he had
destroyed. But the risk of civilian casualties and the need for proof
that the mastermind of al Qaeda was actually dead prompted a
change in plans. The Commander in Chief of the world's most

powerful nation turned to the only team he could trust—our country's most elite and lethal special operations force: the United States Navy SEALs.

It has been said that Bin Laden was already dead the minute the Navy SEALs were called in—he just didn't know it yet. That's because Navy SEALs (an abbreviation for Sea, Air, and Land) are trained to deliver intensely specialized fighting capabilities beyond the scope of other military forces. "When there's nowhere else to turn, Navy SEALs achieve the impossible through critical thinking, sheer willpower, and absolute *dedication to their training,* their missions, and their fellow Special Operations team members." [29]

Finally, the green light was given, and in the early morning hours of May 2, a team of operators known as SEAL Team 6 touched down at bin Laden's Abbottabad compound in two Black Hawk helicopters. They stormed through the ground floor doors of the three-story main building, fighting their way to the third floor where they discovered the most dangerous man on earth hiding in a bedroom.

The SEALs ordered him to surrender. When he refused, two bullets struck bin Laden in the head and chest, killing him instantly. In less than 40 minutes, the operation was over. The world's most menacing figure was no longer a threat. Justice had been served, and the world became safer thanks to a highly trained team of American heroes.

YOU ARE A HERO IN THE MAKING

You may not feel like the kind of hero that could storm a secure compound and defeat a terrorist, but God has a plan to make you a hero of your own unique kind. A hero can be anyone who overcomes his or her weaknesses and rises up to do great things because they have the right cause. Every man, woman, and child on earth was created for this kind of greatness, whether or not they ever become famous. If you believe His promises and trust His power, then

You and your team are called to be heroes of faith.

"'For I know what I have planned for you,' says the LORD. 'I have plans to prosper you, not to harm you. I have plans to give you a future filled with hope.'" JEREMIAH 29:11 NET

"But you are a chosen race, a royal priesthood, a holy nation, a people for his own possession, that you may proclaim the excellencies of him who called you out of darkness into his marvelous light." 1 PETER 2:9 ESV

"Very truly I tell you, whoever believes in me will do the works I have been doing, and they will do even greater things than these, because I am going to the Father." JOHN 14:12 NIV

The Bible is filled with the stories of ordinary men and women who faced their fears and became heroes of faith. Gideon started off hiding behind the winepresses, fearful of the Midianite raiders—but he rose up to be a mighty man of valor (Judges 6). Standing before a burning bush, swamped with a sense of his own failures, Moses asked the Lord, "Who am I, that I should go to Pharaoh and bring the Israelites out of Egypt?" (Exodus 3:11-12). But he eventually did lead the children of Israel out of Egypt. And Paul, the apostle of faith who wrote much of the New Testament, confessed that at times he felt so inadequate it affected him physically:

"I was with you in weakness, in fear, and in much trembling." [30] 1 CORINTHIANS 2:3 NKJV

All of us struggle with such feelings. Our broken backgrounds have a way of humbling us. Our limitations can bind us with fear. Past wounds can breed insecurities in us—the sources of our doubts are endless. If God were to announce, "I am calling you to be on my team," we might question, "Why would God call me? Do I have what it takes?" Yet He does call us. To be the heroes God has called us to be, each of us must resolve our doubts and find the God-confidence to rise up in faith.

111

God meets us in the quagmire of our questions and self-doubts. Consider how God met a fearful young Jeremiah and called Him to service:

> "The LORD gave me a message. He said, 'I knew you before I formed you in your mother's womb. Before you were born I set you apart and appointed you as my spokesman to the world.'"

> ..."'O Sovereign LORD,' I said, 'I can't speak for you! I'm too young!'

> "'Don't say that,' the LORD replied, 'for you must go wherever I send you and say whatever I tell you. And don't be afraid of the people, for I will be with you and take care of you. I, the LORD, have spoken!'"

> "...Then the LORD touched my mouth and said, 'See, I have put my words in your mouth! Today I appoint you to stand up against nations and kingdoms. You are to uproot some and tear them down, to destroy and overthrow them. You are to build others up and plant them.'" JEREMIAH 1:4-10 NLT

By calling us to do great things, God confronts the doubts *within us* with His vision *for us*. When we say, "How can someone like me do great things for you, Lord?" our fear is talking—our inadequacy is fighting for control of our destiny. When fear says *I can't*, God says, *"You can, because I will put my words in your mouth."* If we are willing, God will lift us from the pit of our inadequacies and set us in the palace of His purpose.

We each must come to see our inadequacies as a channel for God's power. God saw the quivering Gideon as a valiant warrior (Judges 6:12), the stuttering Moses as a heroic deliverer and law-giver, and the trembling Paul as an apostle of faith to the Gentiles. Others look at us and see our flaws and failings. We look at ourselves and see our fears and insecurities. God looks at us and sees our possibilities!

God takes ordinary people and transforms them into heroes of faith.

112

The Lord does not see us for what we are, but for what we can become. He begins with us where we are, as we are. He knows our weaknesses, failures, and inadequacies. He never says, "Get rid of those weaknesses, and then I'll use you."

God does not call the qualified; He qualifies the called.

Our questions don't disqualify us from God's team. They can actually become an opening for Him to work in us. God said to Gideon, Go in the strength you have. (Judges 6:14). He said to Moses, "I will be with you..." (Exodus 3:12). Paul recalls the Lord's answer to his lingering weaknesses and fears:

> "Concerning this thing I pleaded with the Lord three times that it might depart from me. And He said to me, 'My grace is sufficient for you, for My strength is made perfect in weakness.' Therefore most gladly I will rather boast in my infirmities, that the power of Christ may rest upon me. Therefore I take pleasure in infirmities, in reproaches, in needs, in persecutions, in distresses, for Christ's sake. For when I am weak, then I am strong." 2 CORINTHIANS 12:8-10 NKJV

Peter started out confident in himself, but fell apart when he betrayed Jesus. It was only then, with his weaknesses exposed before the world, that God was able to transform him into the great apostle of the Book of Acts. King David also understood that God was greater than his inadequacies:

> "O Lord, you have examined my heart and know everything about me. You know when I sit down or stand up. You know my every thought when far away. You chart the path ahead of me and tell me where to stop and rest. Every moment you know where I am. You know what I am going to say even before I say it, LORD. You both precede and follow me. You place your hand of blessing on my head. Such knowledge is too wonderful for me, too great for me to know!"
> PSALM 139:1-6 NLT

That same sense of confident wonder belongs to each of us who serve on God's team. This is because of Jesus Christ. As Paul joyfully proclaimed,

> "Such confidence we have through Christ toward God. Not that we are adequate in ourselves to consider anything as coming from ourselves, but our adequacy is from God, who also made us adequate as servants of a new covenant..."
> 2 CORINTHIANS 3:4-6 NASB

When the love and power of God reaches into our darkest moments of self-doubt, it begins to heal us of our insecurities—it shapes us into vessels of His love for a broken world. He places His hand of blessing on our heads and commissions us to go in the strength He provides.

If you are standing at the intersection of your doubts and your destiny, choose to follow the Hero-maker who believes in you. Though you may feel inadequate, His power qualifies you. His strength is made perfect in your weakness. Press beyond your fears and come together with your partners. Together, you are heroes in the making!

WE CAN BE BETTER

In my book *BEYOND—A Vision for Ten Cities,* [31] I share the story of how the Lord gave me the vision to reach cities using a multi-site church-planting model. This unexpected calling began on the afternoon of Sunday, May 5, 2016 as I was at home resting after a busy day of ministry. It caught me completely off guard, and shook my concept of my future to the core. Yet, it was so clear and bright in my spirit that I had to trust it as the Lord's plan. I wrestled with many doubts and questions. But in the end, the Lord met me with His grace, and I have embraced this calling wholeheartedly.

A few weeks after this challenging vision became real in my heart, Kathy and I were resting together on a vacation in Maui. This time would prove to be much more than a pleasant vacation—it too became spiritually momentous, as God gave further vision to each of us. For Kathy, it was the birth of her first book for women, *Unexpected Seasons*. [32] For me, this time was significant because it clarified my path forward in that vision for ten cities, and bolstered my confidence in God.

One day, as I walked along the Maui shoreline, the word "better" popped into my mind. It's an ordinary word, but it felt so fresh and intense, it was as though I had never heard it before. *Better* was suddenly a new possibility in my life—my ministry could be *better*, my team could be *better*...I could be *better!* The desire to catch the meaning of all this prompted a search through the Bible, and I quickly realized that *better* is a big idea with God.

> "So Samuel said: 'Has the Lord as great delight in burnt offerings and sacrifices, as in obeying the voice of the Lord? Behold, to obey is BETTER than sacrifice, and to heed than the fat of rams.'" 1 SAMUEL 15:22 NKJV

> "A single day spent in your Temple is BETTER than a thousand anywhere else! I would rather be a doorman of the Temple of my God than live in palaces of wickedness." PSALM 84:10 TLB

> "And at the end of ten days their features appeared better and fatter in flesh than all the young men who ate the portion of the king's delicacies.... And in all matters of wisdom and understanding about which the king examined them, he found them ten times better than all the magicians and astrologers who were in all his realm." DANIEL 1:15, 20 NKJV

> "Mary has chosen what is BETTER, and it will not be taken away from her." LUKE 10:42 NIV

> "By faith Abel brought God a BETTER offering than Cain did." HEBREWS 11:4 NIV

As I thought deeply about these verses and many others like them, I was encouraged. I was ready to grow and make changes. The passion for *better* grew, and I settled it in my heart:

*I want BETTER—and I will move
toward it for the rest of my life.*

Before that vacation was over, my journal was filled with insights and outlines on *better.* A new course for my future was set with two simple commitments:

First, I knew *I needed to be better.* It may sound obvious, but it was so poignant: God had given me a big vision to reach cities. To see it happen, I would need to be *better* personally—a better leader, a better communicator, and a better equipper. My faith grew as I believed that I *could* be better. It wasn't that I thought there was no room to improve in my life—of course I knew that I needed to be a better listener, a better husband, a better soul-winner, and so forth. But what came alive prophetically in me was that *better was within my reach. I could be better,* and most importantly,

**If I became better, God's vision for my
life could become a reality.**

The other thing I realized before I left that island was that *I had to train my team to be better.* I have an amazing team of men and women that help me lead and run our church. Our team is a goldmine of talent and experience, yet we had never before done what God was now calling us to do. To reach people as one church in multiple locations, we would need to develop our potential and get *better* as a team.

Kathy and I both came home from our vacation energized. She went to work writing her book, and I set out to restructure my life and team so that we would become *better together.* I hired a ministry coach, and entered into a new phase of personal growth. If I wanted my team and ministry to get better, it would have to begin with me.

I started preaching and teaching on *better.* I gathered our leaders together and shared my passion for *better.* Our team caught the vision and we made our Sunday experiences better, our follow-up with people better, and our ministry teams better. We took our campuses through a top-to-bottom organizational health assessment and objectively determined precisely where we needed to get better. I moved staff members into better roles and restructured the way we worked together. We settled on better structures and refined our plan for reaching ten cities (which is also laid out in my book). We even renovated our building and made it better. Most importantly, our team set aside time week for equipping to get better together.

The decision to embrace "better" changed our team.

Let me encourage you, my dear reader. I may not know you, but I believe in you. If you are a follower of Jesus Christ, you have a magnificent call on your life. You are a hero in the making. You may feel inadequate, but know this: Almighty God is not inadequate, and He is ready to equip you to get *better* so you can fulfill His calling. If He can do it for me, He can do it for you.

You can't get better alone, so gather your team and come into agreement. You and your team are full of potential. If you catch the power of becoming better together, God will transform you into heroes of faith.

EVERY TEAM NEEDS TRAINING

How can our teams get better? What is the secret to releasing our potential? The desire to get better is just the beginning. The best teams know that training is the next step. No matter who we are, or what team we are a part of,

Training is the difference between who we are today and who we could be tomorrow.

The Navy SEALs who took out bin Laden were successful because they had the right training. Every Navy SEAL's potential is developed beginning with what is called BUD/S, or Basic Underwater Demolition SEAL Training. According to the US

Navy, BUD/S is a six-month training course that takes place at the Naval Special Warfare Training Center in Coronado, California. It starts with five weeks of indoctrination, and then progresses thorough three additional phases. [33]

I remember first reading about BUD/S training in Navy SEAL Marcus Luttrell's 2007 gripping book, *Lone Survivor*. As Luttrell describes it, phase one is eight weeks of obstacle courses, swimming, running, sleep deprivation, cold, wet, and exhaustion. The discomfort, pain, and sheer fatigue are designed to force every trainee to question his core values, motivations, and limits. Admiral William H. McRaven, former commander of the Navy's SEAL Team 3 oversaw the mission to get Osama bin Laden. He described Navy SEAL training this way: "To me, basic SEAL training was a lifetime of challenges crammed into six months." [34]

Throughout the grueling process, trainees are required to operate in teams. Their training comes to a climax with a grueling test at the halfway point famously known as "Hell Week." In Hell Week, teams are tested to their physical and psychological limits. Before it's over, about two out of every three trainees has called it quits by "ringing the bell"—a dreaded admission that they don't have what it takes to be a SEAL. Those who complete the first phase of the training process are relieved when they hear their instructors shout the words, "Hell Week is secured!"

The few who remain in the program then move into the second and third training phases, consisting of eight weeks of dive training and nine weeks of land combat training. After BUD/S is completed, they go on for three weeks of parachute training and eight weeks of focused SEAL Qualification Training in mission planning, operations, and tactics.

When these future heroes finally emerge, they have earned their Navy SEAL insignia, and can proudly wear them on their uniforms.

Their training has taken them from
what they used to be, to what they are called to be.

WHY TRAINING MATTERS

There is no substitute for the right training. "Every moment of a Seal's life is geared toward the development, education, and honing of the team." [35] Why? Team outcomes matter. Navy SEALs have a job to do, and they must do it well. The stakes are always high, and effective preparation is crucial. As SEALs like to say,

"The more you sweat in training,
the less you bleed in combat."

Perhaps you're thinking, "I don't plan to bleed in combat, I'm just a part of a church ministry team!" I'm with you. Our teams will never face the kind of pressure a Navy SEAL team does, and that's okay. But let me ask: Do you believe your ministry matters? Do you want to do a good job for the Lord and for the people who count on you every week? Do the outcomes of your ministry matter for eternity? If so, your training matters. From the perspective of building healthy leaders and teams, without training, we can't win the battles we are called to win, and we certainly can't get better.

This is exactly what the writers of the New Testament believed as they described the importance of spiritual training:

"Do not waste time arguing over godless ideas and old wives' tales. Instead, train yourself to be godly."
1 TIMOTHY 4:7 NLT

"But solid food is for the mature—for those whose senses have been trained to distinguish between good and evil."
HEBREWS 5:14 HCSB

"For the moment all discipline seems painful rather than pleasant, but later it yields the peaceful fruit of righteousness to those who have been trained by it."
HEBREWS 12:11 ESV

The original word translated as "trained" in these verses is *gumnadzo,* and it is illuminating. Once again, Rick Renner shares his insights:

> "This [Greek] word *gumnadzo* depicts radical discipline. It was the word the ancient Greeks used to portray the athletes who exercised, trained, and prepared for competition in the often barbaric athletic games of the ancient world. It is where we get the word gymnasium.

> "This word...portrays people who want to develop and change so much that they are willing to put themselves through vigorous, demanding, and strenuous discipline in order to bring about change and to achieve the results they desire...

> "There is nothing more thrilling than to see progress in your life. But to get the kind of progress you desire, you will be required to do something more than you've been doing. You will have to say no to your flesh, denying its appetites and disciplining yourself to do what God says even if your flesh doesn't want to do it. This process often feels long and laborious, but afterward when you can see and appreciate the results, you'll be so glad you didn't quit!" [36]

So God says, "Let me train you. Allow my servants to train you. Embrace the process, even though it is strenuous. It will reshape you and make you into what I've purposed for you to be." It may be a sacrifice, but your mission matters, and your training will be worth it in the end.

I'll never forget when I first became aware of my calling to serve the Lord in full-time ministry. I was 17 and ready to take on the world for Jesus! My wise father gave me some crucial guidance: "Son, if you are going to be a minister, I want you to be a first class minister. I want you to be trained and get a full education. Don't take any shortcuts in your pursuit of God's call on your life." At that time, it felt like an education would be overkill. "I'm ready now!" I thought. I look back and chuckle at my immaturity.

Today I'm thankful that my father knew that training matters and that I agreed to take his advice.

TRAINING MAKES IT POSSIBLE

Allow me to relate another story from my early years in ministry. In 1982, God spoke to our church about starting a television ministry. By then I was 21 and had graduated from Bible School. I was a newly married member of our church staff. One of my duties was producing our daily radio broadcast that aired in the San Francisco Bay Area. Pastor Emanuele Cannistraci is my uncle and was our pastor at the time. Every week, I would take his recorded Sunday messages to my reel-to-reel recording studio. There I would edit down the messages, adding some music and voice-overs, and get the finished broadcasts to the station for airing the following week. So when our team began to think about creating a television broadcast, naturally everyone in the room expected me to lead the way.

There was just one problem with this assignment: I had no training or experience in television production. Sure, I had done radio for years, but television was a far more complicated and expensive medium. We'd have to have a complete video recording system in our sanctuary, complete with cameras, lights, recorders, mixers, and video test equipment. It all had to be purchased, installed, run, and maintained. Editing our messages into a weekly telecast would require an editing system, graphics capabilities, sound mixing, and more.

How could we possibly complete this assignment from God? I was naive and inexperienced, but I believed that with the proper training, our dream to reach people through television could be realized. I began by meeting with television professionals at our local TV station. I described what we wanted to do. They must have wondered if I was crazy, but one man took a chance on us. Bob Coletti worked for KICU-TV Channel 36 at that time, and God gave me favor with him. By our next meeting, he had made it his mission to train me to be a video producer. "David, whatever you need, I'm here for you." It was as if he had said those words from Conversation #1 that always signal the start of big things:

"Let's do this together."

Bob was not a church goer, but he became an amazing ally in our effort to create a volunteer-driven television ministry from scratch. He loaned me books, invited me to production sessions and pointed me to periodicals. Getting the right equipment was essential, so Bob connected me with Bill LeVan. Bill had a small video equipment sales company, and he understood our small budget and big objectives. Bill patiently guided us through the process of selecting and installing a complete video production system, and then he painstakingly trained me on everything I needed to know to run it.

We then needed to train our volunteers to do set up and testing, run the cameras, direct, do lighting, and record the Sunday messages. So, Bob Coletti came to our church every week for months, and taught a television production class for our team of twenty trainees. He used a television production textbook he had leftover from his college days. Matthew Green was a church television producer who flew in from New Orleans and put the finishing touches on our training. We kept working, learning, and listening.

Though it was an almost laughable process, we stayed so focused on getting trained that within a year of our decision to do television, we were totally ready to do it. Every position we needed on our team was filled, and everyone knew how to do their jobs. We began to record and broadcast the good news of Jesus Christ to thousands in our city. Together we created over 270 weekly telecasts that led to hundreds of decisions for Christ. I still remember every single man and woman who served faithfully with me on that team, and I will never forget the lesson I learned about teamwork during that time:

Nothing is impossible if you get the right training.

When everything is on the line, it is your training that gets the job done. Marcus Luttrell echoes the importance of training, quoting the words of his Navy SEAL Master Chief:

> "We've *trained and trained* for a reason: to be *better* at the craft of war than our enemy, to use our skill to perform the mission..." [37]

There's that word *better*. When our desire to get *better* leads us to a commitment to be trained, we are on our way to a heroic future.

What about you? Is there something God has put on your heart to do for him? Is your vision bigger than your ability? If you are working with kids or youth, get trained. If you are doing outreach or compassion, make yourself better. If you are leading a small group or a large worship team, be hungry for training. Make it your aim to get better by getting trained, and bring your team with you. Training makes you better. It's the difference between who you are today and who you could be tomorrow. Most importantly, when you are trained, you can complete any assignment.

WHAT IS YOUR GOD-ASSIGNMENT?

There is a place for each of us on God's team, but to succeed, each of us needs the right training. So at this point in our journey, we need to ask, *What kind of training do I need?* and *Where can I get trained?* The answers to these questions depend on factors too numerous and broad to adequately address here. Your unique training requirements would depend on things like:

- What is it that your team does, and how do they need to do it?
- Where might they have gaps in their skills?
- What is the unique context your team operates in?
- What training is required and available to you?

To get started, focus on the assignment God is giving you. I call this your "God-assignment," and as a hero in the making, you need to understand its importance in your life.

Near the end of his life, one of our heroes, Paul the apostle, reflected on his life and calling. As he looked back, he was able to say that he had completed his God-assignment:

> "I have fought the good fight, I have finished the race, I have kept the faith. Now there is in store for me the crown of righteousness, which the Lord, the righteous Judge, will award to me on that day—and not only to me, but also to all who have longed for his appearing." 2 TIMOTHY 4:7-8 NIV

Our God-assignment is a matter of eternal significance. Paul's mention of the "Righteous Judge" and the crown that was laid up for him on the day of His appearing reminds us of a future and final judgment that will accompany the return of Christ. On that day, there will be both rewards—crowns of righteousness for those who use their abilities well and consequences for those who do not. At the end of our journey, each of us will want to look back and know that we have completed that which God has assigned for us to do.

God has an eternally significant assignment for you.

How can we discover what our God-assignment is? Here are some lessons I have learned along the path I've been walking for over 40 years as I've pursued my own God-assignments:

- *Embrace servanthood.* Whatever your assignment is, it must first be about serving God and others. Jesus warned that we must not be infatuated with titles and positions, but instead see ourselves as servants (Matthew 20:25-28). Embracing servanthood is the first mark of spiritual heroism. Always strive to complete your assignments for the glory of God (1 Corinthians 10:31).

- *Consider your unique identity.* You are an awesome creation of the Almighty. When God made you, He gave you gifts, abilities, and unique characteristics. Are you a supporter or a leader? Are you people-oriented person or a task-oriented person? Tell me

124

how God designed you, and I'll tell you your destiny. When we use our gifts and function in our identity, our destiny unfolds.

- *Follow your spiritual passions.* What drives you? God's passion in you reveals His assignment for you: "For God is working in you, giving you the desire and the power to do what pleases him" (Philippians 2:13, NLT). You will be led by the Holy Spirit to the people and tasks that God has planned for you, and one of the best indicators is a God-given desire.

- *Reflect on past fruitfulness.* Success can be a sign that you are in the right slot. If God blesses it when you do a particular job, you may be on to something. On the other hand, if you have tried and tried to thrive in a particular role, and it never seems to work out, don't be discouraged. Be open to change. Ask around. Seek God and let Him bring you into a fruitful assignment.

- *Be open to changing roles.* At times, we may receive a new God-assignment. This could come in response to a change in vision, a change in season, a change in function, a change in location or a change on your team. It may feel scary, but change can be so good when God is in it. A new assignment can bring new clarity and energy to your life, so be flexible and adapt to what God is calling you to do, both now and in your next season.

The other question to consider is where we should be trained. In my own life, the greatest source of training was my local church. I really mean that. Even though I had the privilege of completing three ministerial degrees,

There is nothing like the learning laboratory of a healthy local church.

That's because a healthy local church is made up of healthy relationships, and relationships are the primary way we grow. A healthy local church is the perfect place for you to be equipped to love, serve, and work with others as a team. It is there you will be taught the Scriptures, which are the primary source of our training in God's ways (2 Timothy 3:16). There you will find leaders who love you and can guide you. There you will have the freedom to make a mistake without losing the support you need to thrive.

God has designed the local church to be a training center. Think of it as a spiritual BUD/S school, only much less dangerous! Ephesians 4 lays out God's plan for a healthy church. In the church each of us is prepared to minister and build others up:

> "So Christ himself gave the apostles, the prophets, the evangelists, the pastors, and teachers, to equip his people for works of service, so that the body of Christ may be built up..." EPHESIANS 4:11-12 NIV

Our potential is developed as we become connected to equippers who function in the gifts that Jesus Christ has given them for the Body of Christ. A case in point is Paul's relationship with his spiritual son Timothy. Timothy was a timid young leader who became a heroic church leader fulfilling his God-assignment because of his training in the local church under the apostle Paul.

Most healthy local churches have training courses and some have excellent schools for ministry. In our church, we have graduated over 300 people from IMPACT! School of Ministry, our own ministry training school. This school was not designed as a formal theological seminary—there are many of those that I could recommend. We wanted to develop a platform for all kinds of people to hone their Bible knowledge and practical skills in a local context.

We believe this is what a healthy church should do. If you have access to this kind of opportunity, take advantage of it. If not, there are great training resources available on the internet 24/7. Look for schools, blogs, articles, and podcasts from reputable leaders in the Body of Christ. Many of them are affordable or even free of charge.

REMEMBER THIS AS YOU TRAIN

We have covered a lot of ground in this fifth team conversation on training. We've seen that God has a plan to raise us up and use us, even though we feel inadequate. We can be used by God to do heroic things if we trust Him and make the commitment to be *better together*. We may not be Navy SEALs, but each of us can accomplish our mission if we are willing to be trained. The kind of training we need depends on our "God-assignment"—the kind of job we are doing and the type of team we are building.

Before we wrap up this chapter, let's consider a few final thoughts that will help us succeed in our training for ministry. As you train to get *better*, remember these three things:

1. Training is as much about love as it is learning.

As we've seen, nearly every aspect of team ministry is relational. We have to be willing to relate in a healthy way to build a healthy team. The process of training is much more effective and enjoyable when it is done in the context of love. In fact, love is what gets us through the hard times in training.

Eric Greitens wrote a piece a few years ago in the Wall Street Journal about the Navy SEALs who make it through "Hell Week." He wrote,

> "Almost all the men who survived possessed one common quality. Even in great pain, faced with the test of their lives, they had the ability to step outside of their own pain, put aside their own fear and ask: How can I help the guy next to me? They had more than the 'fist' of courage and physical strength. They also had a heart large enough to think about others, to dedicate themselves to a higher purpose." [38]

Marcus Lattrell has also weighed in on the power of love on a Navy SEALS team: "In death as in life, we stand together, always a family, always a team. The brotherhood never dies." [39]

Love will get you through the tough times. You have to stay focused on your love for God and your love for the calling He's given you. Love the people you are called to serve, and love the team that is serving with you. Love your local church and the leaders who guide you. Love the pain and believe that it will pay off. And don't forget to love yourself enough to invest in your future. Stay passionate and finish strong.

2. *Training is about teachability more than talent.*

It is not uncommon to meet people in church that are talented but unteachable. Some of them may be on your team, and that can be a problem! To get better, you have to be teachable and humble. You have to accept coaching and advice. You have to show up for training meetings and be attentive to your assignments. No one can get better if they believe they have nothing to learn and no room for improvement. Every member of the team should strive to remain teachable and free of any pride that resists accountability or correction.

Years ago I met a cheerful pastor who leads a significant church in Oslo, Norway. Jan-Aage Torp has a humorous but effective way of teaching the well-known Campus Crusade for Christ discipleship acronym FAT, which stands for *Faithful, Available, Teachable*. The saying goes something like this: "True followers of Jesus should be FAT." But as Jan-Aage explains,

> "Many Christians are faithful except when they are needed, available except when they choose something else, and teachable except when they need to learn something. Jesus didn't fool around with His disciples. He was forgiving and merciful, but he required faithfulness, availability, and teachability MATTHEW 11:28-29." [40]

Are you FAT? While you may cringe at the acronym, its meaning is important. If you want to be a great team member, be *Faithful, Available, and Teachable*. And if you want to build a great team, everyone on the team should do the same, no matter how much talent they may have.

3. *Training will test your timeline and tenacity.*

Finally, remember that anything worthwhile takes time.
Proficiency doesn't develop overnight. Be prepared to stick it out
over time. Real training will challenge you. It will expose your
weaknesses. You will be asked to adhere to standards—this is for
everyone's good. Some people resist standards, but even the Boy
Scouts have them. That's because standards raise the bar and make
the team better. Embrace standards. You will fall short at times and
make mistakes. At times you will wonder if it's taking too long,
and perhaps think you should quit. It's okay to feel that way—just
don't ever do it! Be patient and tenacious.

I read a touching story that illustrates tenacity in the training
process. It's about Milla Bizzotto, a heroic nine-year old girl who
conquered the 24-hour Battlefrog challenge – a U.S Navy-designed
obstacle course. [41] Milla had been a victim of bullying at her school
and decided to reclaim her courage through physical fitness. She
was the youngest competitor in the race by far.

Milla was tenacious. To compete, she had to train for nine months,
five days a week for three hours a day. She told the Miami Herald,
"I don't want to play video games...I don't want to do things to
make life easier. I want to be comfortable being uncomfortable."

"She decided the only hero she needed was herself," the article said.
If a nine-year old can do what it takes to complete a Navy SEALs
obstacle course, we ought to be able to stay committed to our
calling, our team, and our Savior. A common saying among Navy
SEALS is, "Everyone wants to be a Frogman on a sunny day." [42] In
other words, don't be a fair-weather soldier. Push through the pain,
and you'll be a hero in the end.

Even heroes need training. SEAL Team 6 became famous for their
heroism in that early morning raid in Abbottabad, but it was their
training that prepared them to succeed. Whether you and I ever

become famous is not important. What is important is that we develop our God-given potential.

You are called to be a hero, so take every opportunity you have to train and become better. Be a life-long learner—never stop training and growing in God. Never let go of your commitment to get *better,* because your training is the difference between where you are today and where you could be tomorrow.

Conversation #5

TALK IT OVER

After you've read the Chapter on EVEN HEROES NEED TRAINING, take a few minutes with your group to freely discuss the questions below. Give everyone a chance to share, and encourage everyone to be honest, authentic and supportive of others. As always, remember to affirm vulnerability and thank those who are willing to share and ask for prayer.

1. The plan to take out Osama Bin Laden could never have succeeded without teamwork. A team rather than an individual is given credit for this victory. SEAL Team 6 is the hero of this story! Think about what we have learned so far. What essential attributes of teamwork had to be present on SEAL Team 6 in order for them to be successful? What barriers to teamwork would they have needed to overcome before being ready for this important and dangerous mission?

2. Heroes don't have to be famous. In fact, heroes are all around us and they usually don't make the evening news. Perhaps someone specific comes to mind when you think of the word "Hero". What makes this person a hero to you personally? What attributes do they possess that make them stand out? Think specifically about their character and commitment to others. Share a little bit about this special person with your group.

3. When talking about accomplishing great things, self-confidence is a term that will inevitably come up. In this chapter I referred to the need for God-confidence. What are the relationship between self-confidence and God-confidence? How are they similar? Different? Consider Philippians 4:13. Is it possible to have both at the same time?

4. I shared several Biblical examples of heroes who had to overcome great personal weaknesses to fulfill their callings. Gideon, Moses, Paul, Jeremiah, Peter, and David all struggled with fear, personal failures, insecurities, and a tremendous sense of inadequacy. Which of these issues presents the greatest obstacle to you fulfilling your calling right now? Spend some with your team time sharing and praying one for another.

5. Most of us have probably never been through anything quite as grueling and intense as Hell Week. Nonetheless, you probably identified with the idea of "ringing the bell". When things get tough and we are exhausted, we are tempted to call it quits. Think about a time when you "rang the bell" and another time when you persevered to the end. How do you feel about these two different experiences? How do you think God wants you to look at your "ringing the bell" experience?

6. Love becomes especially important when a member of your team is tempted to "ring the bell". Read the following Scriptures together: 1 Thessalonians 5:14-16, 1 Corinthians 12:26, and 1 Peter 4:8. What attitudes and actions should a team take when one member is struggling? Considering team goals, how advisable is it for the team to focus inward like this?

7. No matter what your role is on your team, you have tremendous influence in the lives of your teammates. In what specific ways do you think God can use you to help your teammates become the unique heroes He has called them to be? What role does a team leader have in helping members of their team overcome their weaknesses and discover the greatness they were created for?

Conversation #5

TEAM UP AND MAKE IT BETTER

Before you end your group conversation...

- Spend some time with your team talking about your unique God-assignment. Review the questions on page 123. Talk about things like roles, responsibilities, and upcoming assignments.

- God has a plan to take you and your team from what you used to be to what you are called to be. His plan involves an investment on your part. That investment is training. Think about what God has called your team to do. What training do you need to get there? What resources are available? What other priorities may need to be reevaluated? What do you need to believe God for? How do you plan to get the training you need?

Sometime before your next conversation...

- Making the commitment to become better opened the door for tremendous growth and greater success in my life, ministry, and on my teams. It's often been a humbling process, but I don't regret it for a minute! I hope this chapter has inspired you to join me in this commitment.

- If so, take some time to prayerfully reflect on what better means for you personally. What areas of character growth is the Lord highlighting? How can you be better in your relationships? Better in your team roles?

LEADERSHIP TAKE-AWAY #5:

Healthy Leaders Understand the Seasons of a Team

Your team will not be built in a day. It will take time to...

- Build the team's relationships (see Conversation #2),
- Establish team trust (see Conversation #3),
- Develop team agreement (see Conversation #4),
- Complete team training (see Conversation #5), and
- Use the right tools to finish building your team (see Conversation #6).

Healthy teams—like healthy leaders—grow and mature over time. As a team builder, you need to understand what I call *The Seasons of a Team*. Let me explain.

I recently gathered with group of 30 leaders at one of our newest campuses. Most of them had moved from the San Jose area to the Phoenix area, where GateWay has launched another campus. Led by a strong couple who served at our San Jose campus for over ten years, this group was excited—and in need of encouragement. They had been through a lot as they moved to another state to form a "campus launch team" in this new city. The weather was hot, the jobs were not easy to find, and everything about their habitat was new. On top of that, some of their relationships had become strained. We planned a special time together to renew the vision, celebrate the "wins", and get some fresh perspective.

We gathered at our new location for some tacos and fellowship. We laughed and shared stories until it was time for me to say a few words as the Lead Pastor. I told them how important their efforts are, and how vital this special team is. I reminded them why we are investing so much and how focused we are on reaching lost people in that new region. I assured them that God would bless them and make their efforts successful, and I taught them to understand *The Seasons of a Team*.

"Guys, one of the most helpful insights into how teams develop dates back to 1965, when a professor of educational psychology named Bruce Tuchman published a study suggesting that groups go through four stages as they develop. Those stages are called form, storm, norm, and perform. "Tuchman," I continued, "believed that each of these phases is both necessary and inevitable for any group or team to grow and be healthy. These stages help us anticipate and understand what happens as we put in the hard work of building this campus launch team."

"*Form* is the first stage. It is when a team is just coming together to accomplish a goal, or in our case, to establish a new ministry. People are typically on their best behavior in this stage, and often their focus is on their desires and ideas of the future they all hope for. In this first stage, we build connections and begin to learn what the team will look and feel like."

Not wanting to get bogged down in too much theory, I moved quickly to my main point in bringing Tuchman's theory up.

"*Storm* is the conflict stage. Every team has to face the storms that arise between team members who are learning each other's personalities and work habits. The team is still getting adjusted, and issues are arising. The team is uncoordinated, unsettled, and unproductive. There's a lot going on during this stage. The focus must be on establishing trust, healing tensions, and working through misunderstandings." This was starting to connect with our launch team, so I continued.

"*Norm* refers to the "norms" that the group or team accepts. This is the stage where we have achieved team agreement. We agree on our values, processes, and relationships. We've come to agreement on how the team will function, how problems should be resolved, and much more. With these 'norms' in place, the team can move forward together in harmony." I could see on their faces that hope was rising, so I moved through the final point and prepared to pray with them.

"*Perform* is the 'now-we're cooking' phase. When we get there, we've figured out how to flow together in a satisfying and productive way. We are no longer worried about our earlier challenges—we are ready to function in our mission together. We have become a true team, respecting each other, helping each other, and getting the job done well. The team becomes a source of pleasure. Progress is beginning to take place. The team is creative and collaborative. Information is flowing freely, and conflicts no longer upset the team as they once did."

I looked at them sitting there—having put everything on the line to join our launch team, having so much potential in God—and took careful aim at their hearts. "The reason I share this with you is so you won't feel disoriented or fearful when seasons change or storms arise. Every team God ever created had to face the storms. Anticipate the storms, and embrace the seasons of this team. The seasons of your team will make you stronger. Stay together through each of these stages, and trust the process. God is forming you into a team that will make an eternal impact in this city."

As we closed the meeting up, I invited everyone to worship the Lord, especially those who were in the storm. "As we worship tonight, let's invite Jesus to take us through the storms and get us to a place of faith and trust." We lifted our hands and sang together. Tears flowed and burdens lifted as the Holy Spirit gently fell on each person's heart. We went home full of faith for the future, knowing that we understood the seasons of a team.

As a team leader, you are facing a succession of stages and seasons ahead. I encourage you to hold steady and trust the process. God is about to do His greatest work in you.

Conversation #6

NEW TOOLS FOR TEAM BUILDING

"Give us the tools, and we will finish the job."
— WINSTON CHURCHILL

"Pastor David, do you have a few minutes to call me back? I've got some pretty crazy things going on, and I just need some perspective." Kevin had been a drummer for our worship team and a solid member of our church for years. He sounded upset as I listened to his voicemail message, so I called him back later that same day.

"Kevin, it's me—what's going on?"

"It's just everything right now," Kevin lamented. "My wife is still dealing with her emotions about all her health issues. We're struggling with finances, and on top of everything else, today all my tools were stolen off of my work truck. They're just gone—and now I can't even finish my jobs for my customers. I mean, what else can go wrong here? Does God really have a plan in all this?"

Kevin is a contractor, and the loss of his work tools was a huge blow to his business. I had stayed close to him and his beautiful wife Cherie through their long battle with her cancer, and knew about his mounting financial pressures. The discouragement in his voice was not surprising.

"Kevin, I hear you. This is tough stuff, and I'll pray with you for sure. What else can I do?" I asked, hoping to do anything I could to lift his load.

"I don't know, Pastor. I just need some perspective. I know God is good and He is there for me, but it's hard to see how any of this is going to turn out for my good, you know? I mean, all things work together for good—I get that. But sometimes you just wish things weren't so difficult."

"Your feelings are totally normal," I assured him. "But hang in there. I'm not sure how God is going to fix all this, but He is faithful and He will provide for you. Let's believe that He will turn all of this into a blessing. Every problem has a solution, so let's pray together and seek the Lord's help."

We agreed in prayer together on the phone, asking God to restore Kevin's losses and turn his entire situation around. Though it had been a hard season, I sensed God was up to something and a breakthrough was coming for Kevin and Cherie. We talked a little longer before we hung up, and I was determined to keep praying until we saw the answers come.

A week or so later, I ran into Kevin at a mutual friend's 50th wedding anniversary celebration. It was an outdoor party, and the sun was shining brightly. Cherie and the children looked radiant standing beside Kevin, and I was relieved to see that he was smiling as well. There was no sign of discouragement on any of their faces. We hugged and greeted each other warmly. The kids ran off to play, and we sat down together under the shade of an oak tree to catch up on life.

I was curious, so I asked, "Kevin, what's going on with your business—how are things since your tools were stolen?"

"Pastor, thanks for praying," he replied. "It all turned out to be a big blessing. I replaced all my old tools, and I'm way better off now."

"How's that?" I wondered out loud.

"It's funny, I'd had those old tools for so long they had become inefficient," he replied, smiling. "Jobs were taking too long because of my old tools. I didn't realize that until I got the new tools. Now my jobs are going twice as fast! It's like I've got a completely new business."

His words hit me like a thunderbolt. "Kevin, what you just said is amazing. I'm going to share your story everywhere I preach," I announced.

"What? Why?" He wondered how his experience with new tools at work could apply to others.

"Because not only did God answer our prayers," I said, "but He gave us a prophetic metaphor: when we get comfortable with our old tools in life and ministry, we get stuck in no-win situations. But if we let God replace the old tools with new ones, we can accomplish anything."

When we get new tools, life and ministry will get better.

We gave each other a "high-five," laughed, and enjoyed the party. But the lesson of Kevin's new tools stayed with me. How about you—are you ready for some new tools in life and ministry?

In this final chapter, let's talk about seven new tools for building healthy teams. You may be new to building teams, or you may have been at it for a long time. In either case, these tools will make a dramatic difference in your team building experience.

Before I share the seven tools that I've discovered for building teams, I want to introduce you to one of the greatest team builders of the Bible. He is a true hero of faith, and his story illustrates what happens when these tools are put to use.

NEHEMIAH, THE TEAM BUILDER

Nehemiah was a Jewish adviser to the Persian King Artaxerxes around 500 years before Christ. He served in the royal palace at

Susa, a thousand miles away from his ancestral homeland in Israel. The Jews had been conquered and most of them had been removed from Israel 140 years prior, and Nehemiah had been placed in his high position by God.

In God's sovereign plan, Artaxerxes was then allowing some of the Jews to return and resettle their land. At long last, God's people could return to their Jewish homeland. But what would they find when they arrived? What had become of their sacred capital, its proud walls, and its glorious temple?

When the early reports from Jerusalem reached Nehemiah, they were devastating. Jerusalem's walls now lay in burned heaps, and the few Jews who remained were demoralized. The news wrecked Nehemiah. His heart was so broken for his people that he couldn't eat or maintain his courtly demeanor. How could his once proud nation regain its former glory with its capital in shambles, vulnerable to enemy attacks? The king noticed the expression on Nehemiah's face, and probed for an explanation. Nehemiah turned to God in prayer, sensing that somehow he had to return and rebuild Jerusalem's walls.

To see this almost impossible vision come to pass, Nehemiah would need permission and financial help from the king. God gave Nehemiah such miraculous favor that both answers came immediately. Next, Nehemiah would need to pull a team of people together—a team that shared his vision and would work together to accomplish the impossible before they lost their opportunity. Would they follow him, or reject his idea as foolish? Could any of this be done, even if they were willing?

When Nehemiah arrived in Jerusalem some weeks later, no one knew what was on his heart. For days, he surveyed the sad state of the walls and his people, growing even more determined to get things moving. The moment came for Nehemiah to announce his plan. Gathering a group of demoralized locals, he called them to rise up and form a team like no other team in history, saying,

"'You see the trouble we are in: Jerusalem lies in ruins, and its gates have been burned with fire. Come, let us rebuild the wall of Jerusalem, and we will no longer be in disgrace.' I also told them about the gracious hand of my God on me and what the king had said to me. They replied, 'Let us start rebuilding.' So they began this good work." NEHEMIAH 2:17-18 NIV

Miraculously, the local Jews got behind the vision and came together as a collaborative team. As the massive effort progressed, Nehemiah and his team would battle ridicule, confusion, discouragement, and exhaustion. Yet in one of the greatest success stories in the Bible, Nehemiah's team finished the job in just 52 days! The walls and gates of Jerusalem were rebuilt, and their capital was secure again.

Nehemiah was a phenomenally successful team builder. His team was untested and demoralized, but he rallied them. His adversaries fought him incessantly, but he inspired his team to persevere. The task was massive and exhausting, but they completed it in record time.

Nehemiah had the kind of character that God seems to bless over and over again in Scripture. He was humble and dependent on God, yet bold. He was a visionary and yet a man of the people. He was a warrior, but he knew how to avoid an unnecessary fight. His focus was unbending, and his devotion was unwavering. Nehemiah was a world-class team builder—one that can inspire each of us to build healthy teams today.

SEVEN TOOLS FOR BUILDING TEAMS

Having set the story of Nehemiah's team-building skills before us, we are ready to examine the tools he used. Let's keep a few important thoughts in mind as we begin.

First, team building is a challenging process that takes the right tools. The famous Greek philosopher and mathematician Archimedes is often quoted as saying, "Give me a lever and a place to stand and I will move the earth." With the right tools, we can do anything. These seven team-building tools are powerful, but building a healthy team is never easy—it will require energy, time, and the grace of God. View these tools and the life of Nehemiah as a starting point.

Secondly, these are tools that any team builder can use. If you are a leader, these tools will empower you to build your team. But even if you don't see yourself as a *leader*, I hope you will still see yourself as a *team builder*. Though you may not be as responsible for building your team as your leader, you are an invaluable asset in the process of making your team better. Get to know how these tools work. Read on—everyone will benefit by understanding what tools a team builder values most.

TEAM BUILDING TOOL #1:
Prayer births the team

As a team builder, your first priority is to pray. Nehemiah prayed from the first moment of his plan—long before he even had a team or the permission to rebuild the wall.

> "The king then asked me, 'So what do you want?' Praying under my breath to the God-of-Heaven, I said, 'If it please the king...send me to Judah, to the city where my family is buried, so that I can rebuild it.'" NEHEMIAH 2:4 MSG

This is the second of twelve prayers we find in the book of Nehemiah. Nehemiah's story is filled with powerful, persistent prayer, often accompanied by fasting. Part of what made Nehemiah's prayers so effective is that he was praying based on God's promises. Nehemiah was familiar with the prophecies of Isaiah and Jeremiah. He knew God had promised His people would one day return and rebuild their nation. For example:

> "Your people will rebuild the ancient ruins and will raise up the age-old foundations; you will be called Repairer of Broken Walls..." ISAIAH 58:12 NIV

After Nehemiah prayed, the King gave him everything he needed to rebuild. God will do the same for anyone who prays with faith in the promises He has made.

If you want to create a healthy team, birth it in prayer.

Jesus also modeled prayer as the first step in the building of a team (see Luke 6:12-13). Why would a team builder need to use the tool of prayer? Prayer is the starting point for team building—and everything else we do in life—because it is catalytic. Without God's power, we can never be successful.

There are a thousand excuses not to pray—I know, because I have used them all! We are too busy, too tired, too discouraged, and have too many problems to solve. Yet as team builders, there are some compelling reasons to pray, no matter what our excuses may be.

- *We have a big responsibility.* Think about what God has called you to do. It may not be as big an undertaking as Nehemiah's, but can anything worthwhile be accomplished without prayer? If it is God's work, we must do it God's way. As team builders, we have been entrusted with an awesome responsibility, and it must drive us to our knees.

- *We will face vicious spiritual attacks.* Like Nehemiah, we will be attacked as we try to build. Our health, our minds, and our team will all take fire from the enemy. Through prayer, we put on the spiritual armor that repels the weapons of our enemy and empowers us to stand victorious in the end (see Ephesians 6:10-16). Prayer is the key to spiritual victory!

- *Things are constantly changing.* Times and trends change quickly, and what worked yesterday may not even come close today. If we try to build based on the popular trends, we'll soon fail. But if we build on prayer, our work becomes eternal and we will never become irrelevant.

What can we pray for as we build our team? We can pray for God to send us the workers we need. Jesus directed us to "Ask the Lord of the harvest, therefore, to send out workers into his harvest field" (Matthew 9:38, NIV). We can also pray that the Lord will open our eyes to potential team members, give us His heart for the team, and guide the direction of the ministry. We should certainly pray for our team members to be blessed, rewarded, and encouraged as they serve. And we can pray for our team's efforts to make an eternal difference in the lives of men, women, and children.

The tool of prayer is the first one each of us should put to use—and one we must continue to rely on throughout the process of building our team.

TEAM BUILDING TOOL #2:
Recruiting attracts the team

As a team builder, your biggest role is not to do the work—it is to find the right team members who will do the work with you. See yourself as a talent scout. Look for great people—those special men and women that God has called to be on your team, and draw them together. As you do, keep one thing in mind:

Everybody wants to make a difference.

Nobody wants to be a nobody, and everybody wants to be a somebody. Joining a team is an opportunity to find meaning and purpose in life. The best team builders understand that and leverage it as they recruit. They are constantly communicating purpose: "Here's what we do and here's why it's important that we do it."

When Nehemiah stood over those burnt stones and announced his vision to the locals in Jerusalem, he was recruiting like a master. He arrived virtually alone, and he certainly couldn't do what he needed to do without a team. Surely he was feeling overwhelmed and wondered if people would respond to his appeal. He was an outsider and a palace official. What did he know about the needs and hopes of the locals? But Nehemiah overcame his doubts and stepped out in faith, impressing everyone with the importance of the job and the necessity of joining his team.

There are three important steps every team builder must take in the early stages of their mission:

- *Calling:* The team builder makes a wide appeal to identify those with interest in the team.

- *Selecting:* The team builder screens and chooses his team from among those who respond.

- *Placing:* The team builder gives his or her selections their assignments on the team.

When Jesus recruited Simon Peter and Andrew, he appealed to them using vivid, relatable terms. He promised to make them into "fishers of men" (see Matthew 4:19). Using His metaphor, in the *calling* phase, we must "cast our nets wide" to see what potential team members we can "catch." Once we pull in the catch, we enter the *selecting* phase, where we separate the desired "fish" from the undesired. In our context, not everyone who responds will enhance the team, so selection is key. Jesus said, "For many are called, but few are chosen" (Matthew 22:14). Finally, with the right "fish" selected, they are cleaned, cooked, and served—*placed* in the position to meet the ultimate need.

In the first phase of recruitment, we need to persuade our prospective team members of the importance of the team. Nehemiah did this with a brilliant speech inviting the local Jews to join him. Notice how he moved the hearts of his listeners:

- *He pointed out the problem and the need,* describing "the trouble we are in" (2:17). There is a sense of urgency and destiny about the moment. Great team builders make the case that something has to be done. For example, recruiting people to help with youth ministry becomes easier when you paint a picture of the state of today's youth and everything they are facing. Define the need and point to God's will in the matter.

145

- *He cast a vision of what could happen to meet the need:* "Let us rebuild the wall..." (2:17). This is the "ask"—the call to action that must be a part of every effort to engage new people. Be direct. Invite people to get involved with the vision. Be personal—Jesus didn't rely on announcements. He approached people individually and asked them to follow Him. As a team builder, paint a picture of the future you see as people work together.

- *He assured them of their future success,* promising that "the gracious hand of God" will guide the effort, and that "the God of heaven will give us success..." (Nehemiah 2:20, NLT). This kind of magnetic faith and confidence is essential to great recruiting. Everyone wants to be on a winning team. Don't just state the need—convince people that the team is the way God will meet it.

This kind of communication is called "vision casting," and it is the heart and soul of recruiting. God's people need a clear vision to rise up and do what needs to be done. Good team builders, like Nehemiah, know how to engage people's hearts and move their feet and hands.

The tool of recruiting is one you should constantly use to keep your team filled with the right people. Stop recruiting and eventually you'll have no team, because time and attrition erodes even the finest teams. Stay vigilant and always look out for those who might respond to the call to join your team.

TEAM BUILDING TOOL #3:
Selecting the right people assembles the team

As a team builder, you must care enough about your mission to select the right people. Your team is your future. Make sure you create the right future by choosing the right people.

After Nehemiah prayed and cast his vision, he selected his team and put them to work. He engaged both ordinary people and people of higher station. The enemy viewed them as a "bunch of poor, feeble

Jews" (Nehemiah 4:2), but Nehemiah saw them as heroes of faith.

> "We kept at it, repairing and rebuilding the wall. The whole wall was soon joined together and halfway to its intended height because *the people had a heart for the work.*"
> NEHEMIAH 4:6 MSG EMPHASIS ADDED

Nehemiah picked the right people and built one of the most remarkable teams ever assembled.

Jesus also carefully selected His team members. He didn't hold open auditions and then cast whoever tried out. He prayed over his choices and then approached them individually.

As you build your team, keep the following five C's of team selection in mind:

- *Character* - Are they healthy inside? Do they have integrity? Can they handle conflict? Do they work well with both leaders and peers? Are they faithful or flaky? Living in sin or in humble reliance on God? Do they love the church, the team, and their family in a balanced and healthy way? Character counts more than anything else on a team.

- *Commitment* - True commitment is not about how much time or effort people put into work—it is a measure of how long they will stay with the team. If you select the right people, your team will stick together through the hard times. People who move around too much, or who see your team as a stepping-stone in their larger journey, may lack the level of commitment you need to build on. Look for stable, faithful people who have a record of solid commitment.

- *Competence* - Do they have the skills the team needs? What have they achieved, and what are they capable of achieving? Passion is great, but passion without capability is useless. Look for those who have the specific ministry skills your team needs—or those who can quickly acquire them. Make sure they also have the people skills that make them safe and competent partners.

- *Capacity* - Are they suited to the task at hand? Are they bearing good fruit? *Ability* is key, and someone who can't sing shouldn't be on the stage with a microphone. But capacity also has to do with *availability*. A stressed out person who is barely surviving life's challenges will have a hard time helping you build your wall. Are they able and willing to put the time in? We once had a team member who was capable and really wanted to serve. But she loved to travel and took trips so often that she was virtually unavailable. Great team members are both *able* and *available*.

- *Chemistry* - Do they fit in well with the team? Do they add a spark, or drain the life out of everyone? The ingredient of affinity is crucial to teamwork. Without that relational unison, it's hard to have a great symphony. Watch the relationships with other team members, perhaps during a trial period. When a team has great chemistry, conflict is minimized, work is more enjoyable, and people tend to stay on the team.

After you have selected your team members, place them into their positions. As you do, keep your assignments flexible, and don't be afraid to move people around as circumstances warrant it.

Nehemiah did this because things changed day by day. As people grow and develop, they may become more valuable in another slot. As the enemy changes his tactics, you may need to move team members to reinforce a vulnerable area.

Once you select and place your team members, you are halfway there. You'll still need to give them clear expectations and individual attention. But if you invest in a person who has been poorly selected, you'll eventually regret it. Selection is one of your most valuable tools in building a healthy team.

TEAM BUILDING TOOL #4:
Clear expectations guide the team

As a team builder, you must continually communicate what the team will accomplish and how they will work together to accomplish it. People need to know what is expected of them. They need to see the target of attitudes, behaviors, and outcomes at which the team is aiming.

Nehemiah was a great team builder because he provided clear expectations for his team. He had no illusions about the enemy, the task, or the need. First, he had a clear grip on *the present reality* they were facing—the desperate needs of the city, the honest truth of their situation, and the spiritual source of his calling. Nehemiah also communicated *the task* with clarity. For this hero of faith, the job boiled down to three simple words: *rebuild the wall.* Finally, Nehemiah was clear about *the goals and processes* required to finish the wall. He gave clear instructions and set attainable goals (e.g., Nehemiah 2:3-5).

Without clarity, progress is improbable.

When people know what is expected, they work with less stress, more confidence, and greater synergy. Without clear expectations, people will become frustrated and tentative in their commitment and the team will flounder.

Here are some practical ways any team builder can help create clear expectations on a team:

- *Define the purpose of your team.* Why does your team exist? How does it fit into the larger context around it? What would be missing if your team did not function effectively? Don't be worried about setting the bar too high. People lose interest if they feel they're not being used to their potential.

- *Know your team values and rehearse them.* What should we fight to protect as we do this job together? What should our motives be on the team? What does God's word say about this area of ministry? Constantly monitor your team's performance against your team values, and address any gaps.

- *Provide clear job descriptions.* Everyone on the team needs to understand their role and the requirements of being on the team. Privately compare their performance against the role. What outcomes are you looking for? A one-page job description goes a long way in clarifying expectations on your team.

- *Carefully equip your team.* As we saw in Conversation #5, every team needs training. A team lives or dies based on the clarity and relevance of its training. Design your team as a great habitat for personal growth, rather than a place where people grow stale and get stuck. As a team builder, you are responsible to be sure everyone is clear on how to get better together.

- *Continually reinforce the "why?"* Build team clarity by emphasizing the specific thinking behind your expectations. The *what* informs the team; the *why* motivates and inspires them. Any policies, practices, or changes should be done *with* your team—never *to* your team. No one wants to serve on a team where confusing edicts come down from a team leader's ivory tower.

- *Address team performance.* Great teams work hard to create a consistently high level of performance. When it comes to poor performance, we don't get what we preach, we get what we tolerate. There are gracious ways of handling low performers (more on this in *Leadership Takeaway #6* at the end of this chapter). First, identify the issue — is it character, competence, chemistry? Then talk honestly with them. They may need encouragement, redirection, training, new placement, or as a last resort, to leave the team. Deal with low performers so high performers will stay motivated, and the team won't be dragged down and create an extra load on high performers.

- *Don't micromanage.* Make sure you're not micromanaging your team. Pastor Jacob Stewart is a friend of mine from Hawaii. He recently shared the following definition of micromanager with a group of international leaders:

> "Micromanager: A person who is driven by fear and anxiety into meddling with others' work. Micromanagers are bosses or peers who constantly seek to usurp the decision rights of others. Their excessively insecure and competitive nature causes them to react negatively to ideas and efforts not their own. If they possess authority, they will aggressively use it to control the way work gets done around them. They are typically more focused on process than on the results. They criticize others far more frequently than they praise them."

Jacob wisely emphasized that effective team leaders give their teams the tools they need and then supervise from a distance. They provide feedback at the right times and give each member of the team the freedom to do his or her job. Good teams keep their eye on the results more than methods.

- *Lead by example.* The best way to clarify expectations is through your personal example. If you want your team member to be faithful, be faithful. If you want them to be generous, courageous, and humble, model those qualities for them.

When a team understands what is expected of them, they are not far from success. But there is more to a team than productivity. Teamwork is about relationships, so let's get another important tool in our team building toolbox.

TEAM BUILDING TOOL #5:
Personal attention develops the team

As a team builder, you have a responsibility to care for everyone on your team. Great team builders don't just think about the job— they think about the people who are doing the job. If you don't show up for a few days, things will probably be okay. If your team doesn't show up for a few days, it could be disastrous. Value your team and take good care of them!

Nehemiah saw his team members as family. His story opens up with a conversation in Susa between Nehemiah, Hanani, and some others whom Nehemiah called "my brethren" (Nehemiah 1:1-2). Notice the relational overtones in their dialogue. Nehemiah wanted to know, "How's it going? What's happening in your world?" His brethren opened up and shared their struggle: "We're in trouble. Everything's falling apart." Nehemiah then "sat down and wept." He was a relational leader.

Though he was a palace official, Nehemiah identified with common people, using terms like "we" and "us" (e.g., 2:17-20). This kind of personal connection raised the levels of trust on his team and helped them to accomplish their mission despite opposition and hardship.

Assess your team's personal attention factor by asking the right questions. Does the culture on this team promote strong, personal relationships? Do people feel a personal connection to you as a leader?
Are you building relationships, or just accomplishing tasks?

Keeping people and tasks in proper balance insures team health.

There are at least three motives a team builder has for personally caring for his or her team:

- *Our team is about people.* How can we have a healthy team if we don't love and take care of our team members? Ministry is about people, not positions. Don't see your team merely as a means to an end. Love them as Christ loves them. It's not that you have to drop what you are doing and meet their every need—that's not Biblical. But as a team builder, you can care for your people as you work with them. Personal attention is not a distraction—it is central to your mission.

- *Our team will be attacked.* Do you believe in spiritual warfare? It's real. As soon as Nehemiah's rebuilding project began, Sanballat, Geshem, and Tobiah (all enemies of the Jews) showed up to oppose the work. They used every trick in the book, including intimidation, angry threats, and clever distractions to try to stop the work. Nehemiah stood his ground, armed his people, and kept on rebuilding.

  We too have an enemy who wants to attack our team.

  > "Be alert and of sober mind. Your enemy the devil prowls around like a roaring lion looking for someone to devour. Resist him, standing firm in the faith, because you know that the family of believers throughout the world is undergoing the same kind of sufferings." 1 PETER 5:8-9 NIV

  Our enemy will show up and use every trick to discourage, distract, and defeat our teams. When that happens, don't be idle or indecisive. Pick up your weapons, put on your spiritual armor, and fight (Ephesians 6:10-17). If you lose your team to an attack of the enemy, you lose a lot.

- *Our team needs to stay together.* Having strong trust and healthy relationships lowers the likelihood of people walking away. To paraphrase something that John Moore lays out in his book *Tribal Knowledge,*

  > *"People don't quit organizations—they quit people."*

  What this means is that we are vulnerable to losing good people if we don't bother to personally care for them. If someone leaves your team hurt or neglected, the team member is not at fault—the team builders are. Losing a team member because they have been neglected is a painful tragedy that can be avoided by creating a culture of care on the team.

  There are at least four ways a team builder can pay personal attention to the members of his or her team:

1. Coach their performance.

Once you train your team, be sure to follow through with good coaching. Coaching is the art of helping your team to make the needed adjustments in their attitudes and behaviors. It is reminding your team of what they learned in their training, and it is a powerful way to boost their growth. Coaching works best when it is done with fairness, firmness, and friendliness.

2. Encourage their progress.

Nehemiah encouraged his team when they came under attack (Nehemiah 4:14). Catch people doing the right thing. Let them know they did a great job, and they'll keep doing it. And when they face setbacks or make mistakes—as they often will—be sure to speak encouraging words. There is no excuse for failing to encourage your team. Encouragement is easy and free, so make sure you do it often.

3. Invest in their potential.

People want to work with those who see their potential. I had a pastor who believed in my potential and gave me his best. His faith in me was pivotal in my personal growth and one reason I've stayed with our ministry team for over 40 years. Do you believe in the potential of your people? If so, do they know? When we bring our team to a conference, or simply share a good book or podcast with them, it speaks volumes. People excel when they see us nurturing the seeds of greatness in them.

4. Shepherd their personal life.

The job your team does is important, but it's not as important as their individual spiritual growth. Don't forget your team member's desire to know and follow Jesus. Share what God is doing in your life, and ask them often about what He is doing in theirs. Give them scriptures, pray for them, and be sensitive to their spiritual needs. As a team builder, be a friend in their spiritual development

154

and a support to their spiritual needs.

More than anything, make your team about relationships. Human beings need to feel connected to other people, and if your team meets that need, it will flourish.

TEAM BUILDING TOOL #6:
Pruning protects the team

As a team builder, you must be willing to protect the health of the team by pruning when it is needed.

Some time ago, a friend recommended Dr. Henry Cloud's *Necessary Endings.* [43] I had read some of Dr. Cloud's other works, and this title was so intriguing that I dove right in to it. This is when I first discovered the concept of pruning.

Cloud uses the helpful metaphor of a skilled gardener caring for a rosebush. To summarize, good gardeners know that pruning is an essential part of protecting rosebushes from disease. When branches become diseased, wise gardeners first try to nurture them back to health. If this doesn't work, they must cut away the sickly branch before it consumes too much energy or possibly spreads its disease. A dead branch must also be pruned, as it will take up needed space and prevent new life from growing in its place.

Nehemiah understood this principle. Throughout the Book of Nehemiah, we see him confronting, correcting, and at times removing his own people in order to keep things healthy (e.g. Nehemiah 5:1-19, 13:4-10, and 15-30). Clearly, Nehemiah was not afraid to prune. He was not only a rebuilder—he was a reformer.

The greatest team builder in history
prunes for productivity.

"Every branch in me that does not bear fruit he takes away, and every branch that does bear fruit he prunes, that it may bear more fruit." JOHN 15:2 ESV

155

Just like rosebushes, our teams need care, attention, and careful pruning to flourish. There are times when our efforts to redeem a project, practice, or even a team member may not succeed. When appropriate, a wise team builder gets out the pruning shears and lovingly removes the danger.

Again, the words of Jesus give special insight into this process:

> "A man planted a fig tree in his garden and came again and again to see if there was any fruit on it, but he was always disappointed. Finally, he said to his gardener, 'I've waited three years, and there hasn't been a single fig! Cut it down. It's just taking up space in the garden.'
>
> "The gardener answered, 'Sir, give it one more chance. Leave it another year, and I'll give it special attention and plenty of fertilizer. If we get figs next year, fine. If not, then you can cut it down.'" LUKE 13:6-9 NLT

Notice that the man desired to see figs but he was disappointed time after time.

Continual disappointment can signal that something needs to be pruned.

Seeing no figs, rash action was the owner's first inclination. The first solution was extra attention and fertilizer. A greater investment had to be made to get the desired result. If a greater investment doesn't revive the project, as a last resort, radical cuts must be made.

Finding and cutting away what chokes and endangers our team is smart, though rarely pleasant. Cutting a cherished practice or person from the team will take courage. You'll need a greater commitment to the health and success of the team than to its comfort. While the cut may be painful at first, in the end it will make room for greater fruitfulness.

Pruning is the second hardest thing a team builder will do.
The hardest thing is losing a team because it was neglected.

Don't just build—continually prune and reform. Regularly review everything on your team with an eye toward making needed cuts. Look at habits, attitudes, budgets, schedules, team commitments, and even team members. If it is ailing, fertilize it. After fertilizing with extra attention, if it's still not bearing fruit, or is endangering the team, cut it down and replace it with something healthy.

The ultimate act of team pruning is a complete team shutdown. Sometimes a team has been so neglected or otherwise broken that it is beyond repair—team health is irretrievable, and it is time for what Dr. Cloud calls a "necessary ending." If that is the case, be wise and brave, knowing that,

God has a time for every task and every team.

"For everything there is a season, and a time for every matter under heaven: a time to be born, and a time to die; a time to plant, and a time to pluck up what is planted; a time to kill, and a time to heal; a time to break down, and a time to build up..."
ECCLESIASTES 3:1-3 ESV

TEAM BUILDING TOOL #7:
Celebration rewards the team

The last of our seven tools for team building is far more enjoyable than pruning. As a team builder, you'll want to celebrate with your team as a way to reward them and encourage future commitment.

If you've ever seen a Super Bowl, you know that the best teams in the world know how to celebrate their victories and honor their team members. There are chants, shouts, arm waving, dancing, trophies, rings, confetti, and trips to Disneyland. The celebrations go on and on because great teams know how to celebrate and reward their team members!

We see this tool embedded into the story of Nehemiah. When the wall was dedicated, Nehemiah hosted a huge dedication celebration in Jerusalem (see Nehemiah 12). There was joy and music, choirs and parades, food, and lots of noise! Men, women, and children all came together to laugh, eat, worship, and dance. Imagine how this must have made everyone feel. This unforgettable event was a memorial to the hard work of the people and the faithfulness of God.

There was another, more subtle, celebration in the Book of Nehemiah that should not be overlooked. In Nehemiah 3, each and every person who worked on the wall is recorded by name and assignment. While many of us might be tempted to skip over the long sections in Scripture that list people's names (like the genealogies in the Old Testament), it is important to reflect on what these detailed records actually signify. When it comes to the list of workers in Nehemiah's story, we should understand this:

Everyone on the team is important to God,
and everything they do matters for eternity.

The smallest act of faithfulness can make a difference. On God's team, no one is unimportant and nothing is insignificant. As the Scriptures remind each of us,

"God is not unjust; he will not forget your work and the love you have shown him as you have helped his people and continue to help them." HEBREWS 6:10 NIV

"So, my dear brothers and sisters, be strong and immovable. Always work enthusiastically for the Lord, for you know that nothing you do for the Lord is ever useless."
1 CORINTHIANS 15:58 NLT

That is why Nehemiah kept such a careful a record of everything his team accomplished. He was making sure each person's contribution was recorded and celebrated forever. This level of attention and honor reflects the heart of God and the Holy Spirit, who moved on him as he wrote the words that would one day become Scripture (2 Peter 1:21). Talk about recognition and rewards! How great would you feel if your ministry over the last 52 days earned you a spot in the Bible?

Why is it that, in the church, some people think that ministry should not be rewarded and spiritual accomplishments need no celebration—that somehow rewards are shallow or egotistical? Nothing could be further from the truth.

God is a God of rewards. In the Bible, we can find a multitude of verses that describe rewards. Here are just a few examples:

- God told Abraham: "I'm your exceeding great reward." (Genesis 15:1)
- Job said that God "repays man according to his work, [and rewards him] according to his way." (Job 34:11)
- David declared, "In keeping thy word there is great reward." (Psalm 19:11)
- Solomon promised, "He who sows righteousness will have a sure reward." (Proverbs 11:18)
- Isaiah proclaimed, "Surely my just reward is with the Lord." (Isaiah 49:4)
- Jeremiah heard God say "Your work shall be rewarded..." (Jeremiah 31:16)
- The writer of Hebrews declared "God is a rewarder of those who diligently seek Him." (Hebrews 11:6)
- Jesus repeatedly promised great rewards in heaven (Matthew 5:12, 6:4, Revelation 22:12)

Here are three reasons great ministry teams celebrate and reward their people:

1. Celebration brings affirmation.

Anytime we celebrate our team, it delivers a message of positive affirmation. Too often, we take dependable, faithful people for granted. Week after week, our people overcome their fatigue, personal struggles, and competing demands to serve in our ministries. Most of them would not expect or desire recognition, because they are doing it out of love for the Lord and His people. Yet, when we take the time to celebrate their contribution, it can be a deeply healing experience for them. It also builds a culture of honor and appreciation in the church that benefits everyone and releases God's power.

2. Celebration attracts participation.

Celebration is attractive because it is fun. When your team celebrates and has fun, it becomes much more attractive to new people. No one wants to join a team of miserable people, but if your team loves what they're doing and is having a great time while they do it, others may say, "Why not? I'll serve. It looks like fun!"

Celebration is also attractive because it conveys a sense of purpose. People want to make a difference. Celebration is a wonderful way to communicate to everyone that your team is making a difference.

3. Celebration increases motivation.

When we celebrate and build some fun into ministry, it provides positive motivation. It inspires people to stay involved and keep making the sacrifice. Remember, we are talking about human beings, not robots. People respond to rewards. They change, grow, and get better when they are in a rewarding, honoring culture.

This leads to a principle that every team builder should understand:

You propagate what you celebrate.

When we celebrate hard work, faithfulness, and sacrifice, it sends an important message to everyone. It communicates the kind of heart and behaviors that we want to see more of.

How can a healthy team celebrate? There are endless ways to

celebrate, from small to large, and expensive to free. Here are a few simple ideas that can stimulate your imagination and help you build a unique culture of honor on your team.

- *We can celebrate one-on-one.*

I find that a sincere compliment in a face-to-face meeting with a team member is the number one way to communicate your appreciation. You can also text people, post positive words on social media about team members, send them handwritten notes, or treat them to a special gift or lunch.

- *We can celebrate together.*

When you can, plan special parties, events, and get-togethers for your team. Get together with your team. Feed them, have a party, and celebrate the good times. Build celebration into your monthly or annual calendar. As you do, make sure the word gets out through social media. Let everyone know you love your team!

Don't feel bad if you don't have a big budget for celebration. Many of the most meaningful methods of celebrating your team members are not expensive. A box of donuts is cheap, but it can convey appreciation for your team in a delicious way! Sincere praise is never expensive, and it remains the most important thing a team member can receive.

When it comes to the methods we use to celebrate our teams, we should be creative, thoughtful, and enthusiastic. Small praise is uninspiring. Whatever you do, make it count! Your team is worth the extra effort, and you'll never regret honoring and thanking the people that help you make a difference every week. Celebration is the ultimate tool for energizing and rewarding your team.

In closing this conversation, let's summarize the seven tools that team builders use to build flourishing teams:

- Prayer births the team

- Recruiting attracts the team
- Selecting assembles the team
- Clear expectations guide the team
- Personal attention develops the team
- Pruning protects the team
- Celebration rewards the team

You are a team builder, and your work is important. To build a great team, go after the people who have the abilities that your team needs. Don't settle for just anyone. Seek out great team members. Approach them like you believe what you are doing is important. As they respond, place them, train them, and put them to work. God will bless your team with His power, and together, you will rebuild the wall.

Conversation #6

TALK IT OVER

After you've read Chapter 6 on NEW TOOLS FOR TEAM BUILDING, take a few minutes with your group to freely discuss the questions below. Give everyone a chance to share, and encourage everyone to be honest, authentic and supportive of others. As always, remember to affirm vulnerability and thank those who are willing to share and ask for prayer.

1. I hope you were encouraged by Kevin's story and how God took what felt like the final straw of difficulty and turned it into a blessing for him, his business, and his family. Can you find any keys to success in Kevin's attitude and response? How did he open the door that allowed God to freely move in his situation?

2. Nehemiah had to ask both God and man for what he needed to complete his assignment. Think about the specific resources and permissions that are needed to build your team and complete your assignment. What specifically do you need to pray for?

What do you need to ask others for? Who do you need to ask? Do you believe God will grant you favor as He did Nehemiah?

3. Much of this chapter was focused on leaders, and some of you may not identify with that title. However, leaders emerge on teams when they begin to lead without the title or the responsibility. Review the team building tools. Which tools are appropriate for use by all members of the team? How can using these tools help them develop into leaders? Which tools are most appropriately reserved for those in positions of leadership?

4. I have addressed clarity in several chapters because it is so important to the health of a team. Review the clarity building points on page 149-151. Which of these are most essential for you as a team member? How can you help your team leader give you the clarity you need and build greater clarity on your team?

5. No one enjoys pruning when it is happening. Initially, we usually consider it some kind of attack. Reflect on Kevin's story again. This is actually a story of pruning. God allowed something to be cut away so He could give Kevin something better and make him more fruitful. Do you have a similar story of pruning in your life, a time the Lord cut something away and you ended up better off? Briefly share with your group.

6. On a healthy team, each member feels personally cared for by the group and particularly by the leader. On pages 154-155, I listed 4 ways team builders can invest in individual members and show they care. Which of these is most meaningful to you? What other actions make you feel personally cared for? How does this type of attention make you feel about the team and your place in it?

7. In this chapter we talked about spiritual warfare more than once. We do have an enemy and he will do everything to oppose what God is building, and that includes your team. Take a look at Ephesians 6:10-17. Imagine that Paul had been writing about team armor. What can the team "put on" to protect from

spiritual attacks? What would the team helmet be called? What about the shield? The sword? How can you put this armor on as a team and use it to defeat the enemy's attacks? (If you need some help, consult Colossians 3: 12-16)

8. Our flesh naturally resists correction. But each one of us needs it if we want to become better. In the leadership takeaway, I offer some points to leaders about bringing correction with grace, truth, and love. Be honest, do you welcome correction as kindness? Which of these points could be applied to helping us better receive correction so that we can become better and move from where we are now to where God wants us to be? How can you set your heart and mind to benefit from correction?

Conversation #6

TEAM UP AND MAKE IT BETTER

Before you end your group conversation...

- If you only have one take-away from this book I hope it's the importance of prayer. No other single element is as vital to the health of a team. Take some time together and develop a prayer strategy. What corporate goals need to be brought to the Lord? What specific things do you need the Lord to provide? What has He done in your midst for which you can give thanks? How can the team best pray one for another?

- Celebration is a God idea. His love for a good party is seen throughout Scripture and He celebrates our personal and team wins regularly! Having something to look forward to can help team members work together and get the job done even in the midst of unforeseen challenges and setbacks. Take some time to plan your next celebration. What will you celebrate? How will you celebrate? When and where will the celebration take place?

LEADERSHIP TAKE-AWAY #6:

Healthy Leaders Adjust Their Teams with Grace

Have you ever been corrected in a way that damaged or humiliated you? In this last conversation, we looked at the need to address low-performers on our team, as well as the delicate issue of pruning. As leaders, we need to understand how to prune and adjust our team members so that they are built up, not torn down, in the process.

Most leaders struggle to find the balance between over-correction and under-correction. In the past, I have been guilty of coming down too hard on team members when mistakes were made, only to discover my error later. This painful misstep left me wrestling with how to properly address issues and sometimes feeling tempted to ignore things that needed my attention for fear of making another mistake. To grow healthy teams, we need to learn how to adjust our teams members with grace.

Correcting team members properly is both Biblical and helpful.

"To learn, you must love discipline; it is stupid to hate correction." PROVERBS 12:1 NLT

"Poverty and disgrace come to him who ignores instruction, but whoever heeds reproof is honored." PROVERBS 13:18 ESV

"Be careful then, dear brothers and sisters. Make sure that your own hearts are not evil and unbelieving, turning you away from the living God. You must warn each other every day, while it is still 'today,' so that none of you will be deceived by sin and hardened against God." HEBREWS 3:12-13 NLT

The potential dangers of failing to confront or adjust one another are serious: poverty, disgrace, deception, and hard-heartedness. Any of us could be blind or indifferent to our sins and shortcomings.

The very nature of sin is deceptive and destructive. To keep everyone on the team safe, we must at times offer correction.

Correction is good for us because God uses it to free us from our blindness and indifference to our sin. When we correct someone, it's like offering them the medicine they need to get well. When we receive correction, we are actually being healed. Sometimes the medicine doesn't taste good, but if it cures the disease, it is a healthy thing for everyone involved.

Leaders: Do you have someone helping you see your blind spots?

"Let a righteous man strike me—that is a kindness; let him rebuke me—that is oil on my head. My head will not refuse it, for my prayer will still be against the deeds of evildoers."
PSALMS 141:5 NIV

When we are corrected, we can choose to respond in one of two ways: we can either allow or refuse correction. People aren't infallible, so any correction needs to be weighed. However, a right perspective toward correction is that it is to welcome it as a kindness. God is using it to make us more like Christ.

When we refuse correction, we may react by exhibiting *resisting* or *despairing* behaviors. We resist by pushing back, blame shifting, acting wounded and defensive, or redirecting—"Well, what about what *you* did!" We despair by equating correction as evidence that we are awful people, and we get discouraged. Both responses can be emotionally immature and completely miss the benefit of correction.

How does one move from resisting or despairing to receiving correction as a kindness from God? Ask yourself these questions:

- *Do you welcome correction or merely tolerate it?* If correction is a kindness from God to remove sin from our lives, then it is something to pursue, not just to endure.

166

- *Are you easy to correct?* If people hesitate to bring correction to you, it may be because they don't believe it will be well received. Ask a friend, team member, spouse, or parent for some honest feedback.

Here are four keys to adjusting people with grace that I try to remember as I lead my teams:

1. Begin by checking your motives and refining your approach.

> "Don't use foul or abusive language. Let everything you say be good and helpful, so that your words will be an encouragement to those who hear them." EPHESIANS 4:29 NLT

The purpose of correction must always be to build others up. It must never be to vent our frustration at having been offended or disappointed. Leaders don't correct others to get rid of annoyances—they correct in order to benefit others.

> "Dear brothers and sisters, if another believer is overcome by some sin, you who are godly should gently and humbly help that person back onto the right path. And be careful not to fall into the same temptation yourself." GALATIANS 6:1 NLT

Before you go to someone with correction, consider why you are choosing this moment to approach this person. Is it because you are annoyed or offended by their behavior? If it is, you may be more motivated by selfishness than by love.

2. Bring questions and observations, not judgments or conclusions.

> "... You discern my thoughts from afar. You search out my path and my lying down and are acquainted with all my ways. Even before a word is on my tongue, behold, O Lord, you know it altogether." PSALM 139:2-4 ESV

Only God knows another person's thoughts. The rest of us might suspect a person is in sin, yet if we probed and asked questions, we

167

might find we didn't see things correctly.

If you think someone might be in need of correction, begin by asking, "Can I make an observation and share a concern about what I'm seeing?" Or ask, "Were you angry when you said that? It sounded like you were." Whatever words you use, they should communicate humility— that you aren't God and that your perspective isn't infallible.

3. Remind them of God's love and acceptance, as well as yours.

Paul had to bring a lot of difficult correction to the Corinthians, but he reminded them often of his love and gratitude for them:

> "I give thanks to my God always for you because of the grace of God that was given you in Christ Jesus."
> 1 CORINTHIANS 1:4 NKJV

> "I have the highest confidence in you, and I take great pride in you. You have greatly encouraged me and made me happy despite all our troubles." 2 CORINTHIANS 7:4 NLT

If you adjust a team member, be sure to leave them with hope and the assurance that your relationship is secure. Whenever we draw attention to a person's imperfection, we need to undergird them with lots of forgiveness and acceptance. Anything less is unkind and potentially abusive.

4. Be patient if change happens slowly.

> "And we urge you, brothers, admonish the idle, encourage the fainthearted, help the weak, be patient with them all."
> 1 THESSALONIANS 5:14 NKJV

When I think about how I'm living in comparison to my expectations of myself, it really puts things into perspective. I often say, "Please be patient, God is not finished with me yet." I'm not where I once was, but I'm still not where I should be.

As team leaders, we sometimes want a person's behavior to change completely after one conversation. But we know that our own process of change is often slow and difficult. Changing one's behavior takes time and grace. Exercise patience with those whom you adjust and correct. After all,

God has been patient with you.

Adjusting your team with grace brings a blessing that protects and builds people. When we need correction, we should welcome it, not resist or react to it. When we bring correction, we must be gracious, humble, and careful not to judge another's motive or intent. When we give and receive correction in a hopeful and grace-oriented way, we honor the Lord and safeguard His people.

EPILOGUE

"Therefore we also, since we are surrounded by so great a cloud of witnesses, let us lay aside every weight, and the sin which so easily ensnares us, and let us run with endurance the race that is set before us, looking unto Jesus, the author and finisher of our faith, who for the joy that was set before Him endured the cross, despising the shame, and has sat down at the right hand of the throne of God." HEBREWS 12:1-2 NKJV

"Therefore strengthen the hands which hang down, and the feeble knees, and make straight paths for your feet, so that what is lame may not be dislocated, but rather be healed." HEBREWS 12:12-13 NKJV

Assembly instructions can be boring, but they are vital. I recently assembled a set of patio furnishings at my home. I knew the beautiful patio furniture I had seen on the website would look great in my backyard, and I couldn't wait for it to arrive. Delivery day came, and I was immediately reminded that it all had to be assembled. No problem, I thought—how hard could this be? As I opened the boxes, nothing looked like the pictures on the website. I couldn't imagine how it was all going to fit together. Grabbing the assembly instructions, I looked it over quickly. Still no clue. After some time looking for a shortcut, I was still nowhere. It slowly dawned on me:

*If I wanted to get this built, I would need
to study and absorb the plans.*

I sat down and studied the assembly instructions, putting my desire to build on hold. First, understand the plan, I told myself. You have to see how it all comes together, and in what order. As I followed the instructions, each piece of furniture began to take shape. When I got lost, I came back to the instructions and retraced my steps. Eventually, I had the patio set built, and it looks really good!

My dear reader, the ideas I've shared in *Let's Talk About Teams* will help you build a healthy team. But you will need to work through the tedious, sometimes mundane, aspects of this process, leaving nothing out. At times, you may feel lost, but that's okay. Just come back to the instructions. There are no shortcuts, but I promise you can do this.

As you go through this process, I hope you will maintain team-building traction. Traction is the concept of adhesive grip that empowers the act of pulling, as in the grip of a tire on the road, or the grip of a wheel on a rail. It comes from an old French word that means "draw or pull."

Traction enables us to move things forward.

It brings potential into motion. When we say an idea or a movement is "gaining traction," we mean it is beginning to gain momentum, build in intensity, and really move forward. Contrast traction with the idea of *inertia* (resisting movement), *"spinning your wheels"* (using energy but getting nowhere), or *slipping backwards* because you can't achieve traction.

We may begin in a place of inertia and resistance. Before we can generate movement and speed, we have got to get traction.

Traction also keeps us from falling away. I'll never forget a slippery ride I took through the rain-soaked mountains of Benguet in the Philippines. We were doing outreach in distant villages, and the vehicle we used had balding tires. When we hit the mud, we slipped and slid backwards and sideways, barely escaping a precipitous plunge off the roadside to the valley below.

God wants every one of us to have definite traction in our team. Many are discouraged and exhausted due to a lack of traction in ministry, but this can be turned around if we know what to do and then make some key adjustments. As I close this book, let me leave you with some encouraging thoughts from Hebrews 12 about getting traction as you build your team.

1. Identify the Obstacles.

Using the metaphor of a race, the author of Hebrews calls us to run energetically and consistently despite every obstacle. Obstacles are inevitable, and they pose a clear danger to us. Paul addressed the loss of traction among the Galatians, asking,

> "You ran well. Who hindered you from obeying the truth?"
> GALATIANS 5:7 NKJV

Identifying your specific obstacles is essential to regaining traction. What are you contending with in your bid to move forward? The arenas of the world, the flesh, and the devil are good places to start asking questions. What is blocking you spiritually, emotionally, and physically? Be discerning and honest, and a strategy to overcome can begin to form. Remember,

Traction makes use of friction to gain
an advantage for momentum.

You may tempted to think, "My problems are holding me back." But consider this: *without friction, there is no traction.* Resistance actually gives us something to push against. It is vital to our success! To be an overcomer, you need something to overcome. See your place of trouble as a place of opportunity to get traction. Run through your troop and leap over your wall!

Take Action: **Make a list of the most challenging issues you face in ministry.** This is going to be your starting point in prayer, counsel, strategic planning, and work. Create a corresponding list of promises from God's Word and prophetic words to bolster your faith, and review it often.

2. Draw from Prototypes.

We are reminded to draw from the cloud of faith-witnesses that surrounds us—the mighty heroes of faith who overcame their obstacles and ran their race. They model traction in ministry.

God has placed prototypes and examples all around us. They are there in Scripture, history, and present relationships. Let them inspire and guide you as you read their writings and explore their examples. Be sure to set aside time in your schedule to read current articles and books by men and women of proven character that have achieved traction in ministry.

> *Take Action:* **Identify a ministry model that both feeds and challenges you, and draw from it.** With a prototype, you will be able to identify key systems, values, strategies, and cultures that can work for you. Stay true to your unique calling and identity, but don't be afraid to draw from the multitude of witnesses God has placed around you to help point the way.

3. Connect with Catalysts.

For Jesus, the joy of fulfilling the Father's plan to redeem people was the catalyst that energized Him: "For the joy set before Him, He endured" (Hebrews 12:2). What sparks you? What gives you the passion and drive to move forward? Consider a short list of available catalysts:

- *The Holy Spirit is catalytic.* Get refilled and renewed, and stay there. There is nothing like a fresh thrust in fasting and prayer to create traction in your personal life and ministry.

- *Vision is catalytic.* Reconnect with God's picture of your future. Let it hit you inside. Dream and journal about what God has placed inside you. Fall in love with people and work to reach them.

- *Relationships are catalytic.* Iron sharpens iron, and we need strong connections to succeed.

- *Better is catalytic.* Seek to make constant improvements. Never be satisfied with mediocrity or "good enough." Strategic upgrades and improvements create traction in every area of life.

- *Success is catalytic.* Keep up the good work. Nothing breeds success like success. Big accomplishments are rarely the result of a singular event or action, but a series of successful steps. A succession of previous "wins" puts a wonderful wind in the sail.

Take Action: **Embrace key changes that will catalyze.** Being stuck is generally about avoiding change. Welcome anything that has the potential to spark good. Seek God afresh in fasting and prayer. Be open to change, and you will find traction is easy.

5. *Break Free from Dead Weights.*

Hebrews 12 calls us to let go of anything that weighs us down. The writer is careful to distinguish dead weight from sin: "Every weight AND the sin..." meaning they are two separate issues. Not every dead weight is a sin, but if it weighs you down, it's no good.

Most of us are already aware of our sin issues and how they threaten our future. If sin is stalking you, set some boundaries, repent, and move toward righteousness. If sin is ensnaring you, get help from someone you trust.

Your traction depends on your freedom.

The tougher question may be traditions, mindsets, and even people who may be acting as dead weight, slowing you down. Spirit-directed pruning can bring fresh fruitfulness. In my own ministry, I've had to prune away some involvement in peripheral commitments. It was all good stuff, but the expectations were weighty and I was ensnared. When I modified my load, my race became easier, more enjoyable, and far more victorious.

Take Action: **Review everything with an eye toward making strategic cuts.** Look at budgets, schedules, and relational commitments. Is the tail wagging the dog somewhere? As we saw in Conversation #6, if it's not bearing fruit, and hasn't for some time, cut it down and replace it with something that will (Luke 13:6-9).

6. Fix your Focus.

We are reminded that traction comes by "Looking unto Jesus..." (Hebrews 12:2). I once read the story of Tino Wallenda of the famous "Flying Wallendas" acrobatic family. He said,

> "When I was seven, my grandfather put me on a wire two feet off the ground. He taught me all the basics: how to keep my body stiff, how to place my feet on the wire, and how to hold the pole. But the most important thing was to focus my attention on a point that was unmoving. That is how we maintain our balance on the wire. You need a point to concentrate on to keep you balanced."

Fixing your focus on Jesus keeps you balanced and moving forward.

Nothing should eclipse Him as the focus of our lives, much less our teams and ministries. His teaching, example, and living influence can move us like nothing else. Looking to Jesus propels us past our discouragements. Don't let your focus become broken by religion, ministry, fads, negative people, the drive for success, or the need for human approval. Keep Christ central in everything, and you will never lose traction.

Take Action: **Repair any area of broken focus.** More than money, success, relationships, work, school, or sports—a focus on Jesus will fertilize your future and set you up for a harvest. But beyond Jesus, are you paying attention to the important things? Are you as focused as you should be on your mission, your team, and your use of resources, such as time?

7. Get a Fresh Grip.

"Grip" is a defining term when it comes to traction. The author of Hebrews exhorts us to "Strengthen the hands that hang down," or as JB Philips translates it, "So take a fresh grip on life and brace your trembling limbs. Don't wander away from the path but forge steadily onward. On the right path the limping foot recovers strength and does not collapse." (vv. 12-13)

It is interesting to go through Scripture searching for the concept of "getting a grip." The Biblical phrases have to do with "taking hold of" or "gathering up." There are many things that we need to get a grip on, but a few of them really stand out.

- *Get a grip on yourself.* Consider your emotions, faith, spiritual life, and time. If you can't manage yourself, you will never get traction with others.

- *Get a grip on your team.* Are you listening, connecting, and imparting what they need to be successful? Are they on mission together?

- *Get a grip on your core beliefs and principles.* In terms of both doctrine and vision, what is non-negotiable for you and your team? What has God said about your values, community, and calling? It may be time to revisit and revise your mission statement and communicate it afresh to your team.

8. Decide to Persist.

Perhaps most importantly, the writer of Hebrews encourages us to, "Run with endurance the race that is set before us..." noting that Jesus "endured the cross, despising the shame." It was His endurance that enabled Him to finally sit down beside the Father's throne, completely victorious.

Success requires determination,
patience, and proper pacing.

When doing life and ministry as a team, we must move deliberately and wisely, as in a marathon. Think long term and refuse to burn out. Think sustainable effort, not momentary bursts of brilliance between long periods of dullness and inactivity.

Persistence has the power to bring us incredible spiritual victory. Every cross leads to a crown, every trial to a throne. Jesus made it to the Father's right hand because he chose to never quit. I've personally made the same choice—have you? Discouragement is a luxury we cannot afford. There is too much at stake in our world. God has chosen us, and despite the past, we can move forward in our race. If we stay with it, we win.

My prayer for you is that you will quickly get traction with the ideas you have gleaned in these six important conversations. May you and your team flourish as you run toward the prize. Stay close to the assembly instructions, and keep identifying obstacles, drawing from prototypes, connecting with catalysts, breaking free from dead weights, fixing your focus, regaining your grip, and making the choice to stay with it no matter what.

About the Author

David Cannistraci is the Lead Pastor of GateWay City Church, a multi-site church based in San Jose, California. Having served around the world for over 35 years as a pastor, missionary, author, church planter and community leader, he has become known for building an innovative church and inspiring leaders to grow.

David's first book, *Apostles and the Emerging Apostolic Movement* (Regal, 1996) has been widely received as a foundational work on the subject of contemporary apostolic ministry. It has been translated into seven languages. David's second book, *God's Vision for Your Church* (Regal, 1999) explores corporate gifting and God's unique purpose for every church, network and denomination. His articles have appeared in both Charisma and Ministry Today magazines.

David's earned degrees include a Bachelor of Science from Bethany University, a Master of Divinity from Christian International Graduate School, and a Doctor of Philosophy from California Graduate School of Theology.

David and his wife Kathy have been married and in full-time ministry together since 1982. They live in Morgan Hill, California where they enjoy an active life with their two sons, two daughters-in-law and grandchildren.

gatewaycitychurch.org | DavidCannistraci.org | @pastorofgateway

NOTES

[1] David Cannistraci, *Apostles and the Emerging Apostolic Movement* (Ventura:

[2] David Cannistraci, *God's Vision for Your Church* (Ventura: Regal Books, 2001).

[3] Jon R. Katzenbach and Douglas K. Smith, *The Wisdom of Teams* (Boston: Harvard Review Press, 1993), 45.

[4] John Maxwell, *Developing the Leader Within You* (Nashville: Thomas Nelson, 1993) 116.

[5] See Matthew 28:19, 1 John 5:7

[6] Absalom is an example of a failure to leave a legacy: "During his lifetime, Absalom had built a monument to himself in the King's Valley, for he said, I have no son to carry on my name" (1 Samuel 18:18).

[7] "Managing to Minister: An Interview with Peter Drucker" *CT Pastors*, accessed July 29, 2018, www.christianitytoday.com/pastors/1989/spring/89l2014.html

[8] Carl F. George, *Prepare Your Church for the Future* (Tarrytown: Revell, 1991), 129-131.

[9] Patrick Lencioni, *The Five Dysfunctions of a Team* (San Francisco: Jossey-Bass, 2002)

[10] See Alexander Strauch's *A Christian Leader's Guide to Leading with Love* (Littleton: Lewis and Roth, 2006) and Perry Noble's *The Most Excellent Way to Lead: Discover the Heart of Great Leadership* (Carol Stream: Tyndale, 2016).

[11] Adapted from James M. Kouzes and Barry A. Posner, The Leadership Challenge: How to Keep Getting Extraordinary Things Done in Organizations (San Francisco: Jossey-Bass, 1995). Retrieved August 13, 2018 from bible.org/seriespage/team-building#P22_4824

[12] General Stanley McChrystal, *Team of Teams* (Great Britain: Portfolio Penguin, 2015), 96, emphasis mine.

[13] Laura Delizonna, "High Performing Teams Need Psychological Safety. Here's How to Create It," Harvard Business Review, August 24, 2017. Retrieved August 13, 2018 from hbr.org/2017/08/high-performing-teams-need-psychological-safety-heres-how-to-create-it

[14] "Mountain Climbers Help Each Other," Submitted by E. M. Gershater, bible.org accessed August 23, 2018, bible.org/illustration/mountain-climbers-help-each-other

[15] "Offstage and On, Billy Graham's Ministry was a Team Effort," Adelle M. Banks on Religion News Service, Thursday, February 22, 2018 accessed August 13, 2018, christianheadlines.com/news/offstage-and-on-billy-graham-s-ministry-was-a-team-effort.html

[16] Patrick Lencioni, *The Advantage: Why Organizational Health Trumps Everything Else in Business* (San Francisco: Jossey-Bass, 2012)

[17] *GateWay's Worship Culture Manual* (San Jose: GateWay City Church) is available by contacting our offices at info@mygatewaycity.church.

[18] I have a complete teaching called *The Spirit of Separation* that many have found life-changing in their relationships. It is available for free online at davidcannistraci.org/news/2015/12/18/leviathan-the-spirit-of-separation

[19] For an excellent guide on honest communication in a team setting, the author recommends *Crucial Conversations: Tools for Talking When Stakes are High* by Kerry Patterson, Joseph Grenny, Ron McMillan and Al Switzler (New York: McGraw Hill, 2012).

[20] James M. Kouzes & Barry Z. Posner, *The Leadership Challenge: How to Make Extraordinary Things Happen in Organizations* (Jossey-Bass, 2012), pg. 74

[21] Adapted from James M. Kouzes and Barry A. Posner, *The Leadership Challenge: How to Keep Getting Extraordinary Things Done in Organizations* (San Francisco: Jossey-Bass, 1995). Retrieved August 13, 2018 from bible.org/seriespage/team-building#P22_4824

[22] Among others, I recommend Pastor Justin Manzey of Latitude Ministries, www.latitudeministries.com

[23] "How Members of the Symphony Orchestra Viewed Each Other," sourced from Today in the Word, June 22, 1992 by bible.org accessed August 25, 2018, bible.org/illustration/how-members-symphony-orchestra-viewed-each-other

[24] From a message by Ben Patterson, "A Faith Like Mary's," Preaching Today, Tape No. 87.

[25] Rick Renner, *Sparkling Gems from the Greek* (Tulsa: Teach All Nations), 668.

[26] See 2 Kings 4:38ff.

[27] For a good discussion of the purpose of written team agreements from a business perspective, see Peter W. DuPont and Kunal Thakore's "The Importance of Team Agreements" at fourbridgesadvisorysf.com/resources/

[28] Jon R. Katzenbach and Douglas K. Smith, *The Wisdom of Teams* (Boston: Harvard Review Press, 1993), 112

[29] US Navy Seal Careers, retrieved September 2, 2018 from navy.com/careers/navy-seal, emphasis mine.

[30] Some have suggested these are the identical symptoms of a panic attack. Whatever they were, it is clear that Paul was wrestling with deep questions of inadequacy in ministry.

[31] David Cannistraci, *BEYOND: A Vision for Ten Cities* (San Jose: GateWay City Church, 2017) is available at amazon.com.

[32] Kathy Cannistraci, *Unexpected Seasons: Believe and Move Forward into Your Best Season* (Houston: Worldwide Publishing Group, 2018), also available at amazon.com.

[33] "How Navy Seals Train, US Navy Seals" accessed August 12, 2018 at navyseals.com/nsw/bud-s-basic-underwater-demolition-seal-training/

[34] "How Navy Seals Train, US Navy Seals" accessed August 12, 2018 at navyseals.com/nsw/bud-s-basic-underwater-demolition-seal-training/

[35] "How Navy Seals Train, US Navy Seals" accessed August 12, 2018 at navyseals.com/nsw/bud-s-basic-underwater-demolition-seal-training/

[36] Renner, 834.

[37] Marcus Luttrell, *Service: A Navy SEAL at War* (New York: Little, Brown and Hatchett, 2012), 227, emphasis mine.

[38] Eric Greitens, The Wall Street Journal, May 7, 2011, "Navy SEALs Succeed by Focusing on Others," accessed August 12, 2018, preachingtoday.com/illustrations/2011/may/2052311.html

[39] Luttrell, 318

[40] Jan-Aage Torp, "FAT," accessed September 4, 2018, oslo.church/read/fat

[41] Selena Ivanovic, "9-year Old Girl Completed US Navy Seals Obstacle Course," accessed August 22, 2018, novakdjokovicfoundation.org/milla-bizzotto-us-navy-seals-obstacle-course/

[42] Needham, 126

[43] Henry Cloud, *Necessary Endings* (New York: Harper, 2010).

57014362R00114

Made in the USA
Columbia, SC
03 May 2019